Browsing in the
Blackdowns

GW00506938

Sheila Eckhart

**White Tree
Books**

First published in 1991 by
WHITE TREE BOOKS
an imprint of REDCLIFFE PRESS LTD.,
49 Park Street, Bristol BS1 5NT

ISBN 0 872971 07 5

Typeset and printed by The Longdunn Press Ltd., Bristol.

Contents

The Ridge Road, with the avenue of beeches.

Introduction

I listened one evening to the man who had just rowed a boat single handed across the Atlantic. When asked by the reporter why he did it, he replied, "A man's got to have a challenge, and it was there".

We all want to achieve some secret ambition. I want to drop everything and do a really long walk. I have done an odd week here and there, but I am thinking of a walk taking about six months, in some remote unexplored area. That is all very well, but there are other considerations; family, job, money. One just cannot be free to pack up and leave everything.

After listening to the rowing man, I thought I could fulfil a small part of my ambition without a lot of upheaval, so I decided to walk my favourite range of hills, The Blackdowns, from one end to the other, a little known ridge of undiscovered beauty, running from Devon into Somerset, hills and combes rich with forest and pasture, rivers and common. I discovered that not much has been written about them, and I thought my best contribution would be to write about my walk.

Even starting a small project like this, I found, has to be thought about first. Where do the hills start and finish? What will one write about them? I am a fairly seasoned walker and I am never happier than when I am out in the rain with my boots on my feet and a rucksack on my back. The walking was going to be the least of my problems. In England there are 103,000 miles of footpaths; these were mainly laid down anciently. I would walk on a footpath rather than the road whenever possible.

There is some argument as to where the hills begin; different maps give different impressions. The Blackdown Hills have so many spurs that are not easy to delineate. I realised what a huge task I had taken on, so in the end I plumped for Culmstock Beacon in the west to Castle Neroche in the east. I would also cover all the small villages within the shadow of the hills. I drew a circle on my Ordnance Survey map taking in Wellington, Culmstock and Hemyock, then down to Luppitt, and staying on that side of the A.303 except for crossing to Chard, Combe St Nicholas and Whitestaunton. The oldest buildings mainly are the churches, the footpaths are either non existent or poorly marked, and the industry is mainly agricultural. The flora and fauna and the pubs are also not without their variety, so I decided to include anything at all that took my eye, or hopefully was going to teach me something.

Therefore in this book I have set down many treasures of The Blackdowns, which readers may like to discover for themselves. When visiting the churches, it should be remembered that they are our national heritage, being some of the oldest and most elaborate buildings in the land; they take a lot of upkeep, so a small donation in each offertory box would be welcomed. When walking the lanes and footpaths remember the country code.

> Take nothing away,
> Leave only footprints,
> Shut all gates,
> Keep dogs on leads where stated,
> Above all, thank God for the eyes,
> Which enable one to see all this beauty.

One of the locals told me, when I was enquiring about a certain footpath, that if it is not used by the public for a year, then it is no longer a public right of way. This is not correct. A footpath is a footpath until such time as the Council involved decides to delete it from updated maps. If a footpath is blocked a diversion can legally be made, but this does not mean cutting wire or causing damage. Sometimes footpaths run through farmyards and as these are places of work, they have to remain a farmyard in the first instance, and a right of way second.

The Open Spaces Society have recently said that routes of footpaths are being radically altered under the new Countryside Commission proposals. Strings are being attached to the legal requirement that all public paths should be made walkable by the year 2000 AD. At present if a farmer makes a slight change, he has to show that it is of benefit to the public, the Commission proposes that he need no longer do this. According to the Society, users who oppose path changes are already at a disadvantage. The Secretary of the Open Spaces Society recently said "Such a weakening of existing safeguards will be prejudicial to the public in Somerset, as well as elsewhere. Our ancient and much loved paths, which are badly abused by some farmers and landowners, could be distorted out of recognition". The Society wants the Commission to co-operate with highway authorities, in opening up more paths for everyone to enjoy and to drop these unpopular proposals.

The Blackdown Hills are composed of rocks of the Mesozoic era (100/150 million years ago). They are mainly limestone hills and the lime kilns kept people employed for several generations. Blue Lias stone also comes from the Blackdowns in the Corfe/West Hatch area, this had to be mined out rather than blasted, as it is embedded in layers and splits naturally into blocks. Whetstone mining was a considerable industry during the 18th and 19th centuries. There is a 100 foot layer of greensand, with marl beneath it which makes it impervious to water (marl is a crumbly mixture of clay, sand and limestone), consequently much of the lower regions of the hills are often water logged after heavy rain. The Blackdowns are well known for the fossils which are found in the greensand layer. This layer was deposited about 70 million years ago. On the higher regions of the Hills clay with flints and cherts can be found. Flint stone is found in the higher Holman Clavel and central areas, it is used in most of the Blackdown Churches and other buildings, and can easily be seen even in enclosing walls. So the Hills are very wet and consist mainly of clay soil which makes farming hard work. In times of shortage trees were chopped back and more land put under cultivation, but in times of plenty when surplus land was not tilled or grazed, the trees and scrub land soon took over again and turned the terrain back to woodland. The Hills have remained much the same for several hundred years.

The Blackdowns are full of small enclosures with beautiful hedgerows which harbour so many species of wildlife. Many of these were originally earthen walls which kept in animals and which over the years became covered in vegetation. Others were put there in about the 18th century when the open plan system had finished and smaller units came into being. In much of the country hedges are now being destroyed to make way for larger fields and therefore easier work for the heavy farm machinery and this is destroying the habitat of so many creatures.

Family names reverberate across the Hills. These are people who have left their mark over the centuries and have helped to make the history of the area, Popham, Colles, Orchard, Portman, Newton, Wyndham, Simcoe, Combes, Willet and many more.

These hills, like the rest of the country, have not been without the traumas of disease. The Black Death began in Somerset in 1349 and no area was immune from it. This plague took more than half the population of the country with it. It was believed to have been brought into the country by ships docking at Weymouth, then carried by rats and fleas. Orchard House was knocked down because of a typhus outbreak in 1843 and there was a severe outbreak of smallpox in Trull at about the same time.

Before the reign of George IV, suicides were not allowed to be buried in the churchyard or in consecrated ground. Suicides, witches and unbaptised babies were often buried at a cross roads; witches and sometimes gypsies had stakes through the heart, to stop their souls from wandering around. In George IV's reign Parliament passed an Act which allowed such people to be buried in the north side of the churchyard, the cold side. No prayers or religious rights were performed over them. This Act also forbade the use of stakes. There are many ghost stories connected with Somerset and other places, where the ghost haunts a cross road.

Gravestones are another feature I found in a fair variety on the Hills. The very old churches have stone coffins with effigies on top inside the church, or sometimes flat memorial stones let into the floor of the church. Very

7

often they show the cause of death, or even the person's trade. Some have witty verses written on them, but in this book I have only room to mention one or two, as there are so many. On the effigy tombs children of the deceased are usually kneeling around the tomb, if one of these children is holding a skull in its hands this shows that it died before its parents. Later came the family vaults, or table tombs; they are mainly outside in the churchyard and often these days people will be found sitting on them. The next generation of tombstones became elaborate with angels, crosses and coloured chippings, but today, if burials take place at all, the stones have to be plain and stand in straight lines so that the motorised mower can pass between them.

In the very early dark days monks would ride on horseback from village to village to pass on the word of God. They would choose a spot somewhere near the centre of a community and mark it with a cross. After a time a church would be built on the site by the cross; this piece of land would be given by the Lord of the Manor for the purpose. The plot would be consecrated and from then onwards this holy ground would be used for all manner of village activities.

Churchyard crosses are therefore another sign of age. Long before the Reformation a stone cross signified the sanctity of consecrated ground. Many business deals between merchants were fixed by the churchyard cross because no-one would lie or cheat on consecrated ground. The Puritans and Cromwell were responsible for the destruction of many of these, but there are still a few remaining. Churchyard crosses were erected again occasionally in this century as memorials to the two world wars.

Many examples of Stocks, implements of torture in the middle ages, still remain in the churchyards. It was hoped that punishment carried out on consecrated ground would lead to remorse and better future behaviour from the criminal.

It will be noticed that many churches were either rebuilt or restored in the 15th century and again in the 19th century. There are two reasons. First, these were affluent times first with the wool industry and latterly the industrial revolution. Second also at these times the churches had become very run down and were in dire need of repair.

The Toleration Act of 1689 gave non-conformists the right to worship openly and the new Methodist religion became prominent.

I found a wide variety in dwelling houses of the materials used, chert and flintstone, cob, long houses, corrugated tin roofs, thatched roofs and many more. Reed is always much in demand in this area with so many thatched houses. I found such a large number of listed buildings in my chosen area that it became impracticable to mention them all.

In this book I have also mentioned many public houses, hotels and restaurants, because in my search for interesting historical and other facts, they came to my notice. There are equally as many which I have not mentioned. Good food can be obtained in most pubs now, especially in Somerset. They try to serve the needs of the locals, as well as the tourists. I had a meal in most of the Blackdown eating places on my journeys and I can honestly say I did not find a bad one. There are smart looking beer gardens, specialist beers, entertainment for children, family rooms, the quality of such facilities is so high, that it made necessary breaks attractive.

I have mentioned many small industries, but the primary industry in these hills and the one that I have spoken of least is farming.

Schools also feature. In 1870 Gladstone made an Act which laid down adequate elementary education throughout the country.

Most of the time I was able to walk a footpath, but I also walked many lanes, and I am ashamed to say I even got lost in the beginning. Again I found doing a project like this was not, as I first thought, simply walking from Culmstock Beacon to Castle Neroche. It was a question of continually zigzagging, north to south and back again.

The main road which runs along the top of The Blackdowns is referred to as the Ridge Road: It has been a road since the earliest times, gradually getting wider to support the traffic of the day. It was a track and then a drove road until the Romans and then the Saxons came along; they widened it and someone named it Ford Street. In 710 King Ina of Wessex fought a great battle against the King of Dumnonia and the Ridge Road of The Blackdowns formed the border. It is still partially a border between Devon and Somerset.

By the 1660's each village had its "Dwelly's Hearth Tax" returns. This tax had to be paid by anyone owning a hearth. A hearth Tax Exemption Certificate would be given in the following circumstances:—

1. To the very poor.
2. If the house occupied was not of greater annual value than £1.
3. If the house owner possessed no other land or goods over the value of £10.
4. The Exemption Form had to be certified by the Minister, Churchwardens and Overseers. One means of exemption was by bribing these officials.

Hearth Tax or Chimney Tax on every fireplace was levied in England in the form of Peter's Pence during the Middle Ages and was imposed as a National Tax by Charles II in 1662, at the rate of two shillings a hearth. There was exemption for tradesmen and the poor. It produced about two hundred thousand pounds a year. It was very unpopular and was abolished in 1689, only to be replaced by the window tax.

These hills are rural simplicity in its most splendid form. Since I started this walk and cataloguing of The Blackdowns, The Blackdown Society have requested to have the hills designated as an area of outstanding natural beauty (A.O.N.B.).

So come with me as I ramble along these byways and listen to the gossip and the birdsong, the stories and legends.

Chapter One
The Western Hills

Culmstock Beacon: unlike most hills where a beacon was lit, Culmstock Beacon actually has a very interesting little stone building. It is a Trig Point for the O.S. and it has a bench mark S.3745. It was one of the beacons used to warn of the Spanish Armada.

Looking east from the Beacon the top of Wellington Monument can just be seen through the trees. It is an excellent walk of roughly three miles. Setting off east from the Beacon, there is a wide green area, known as Black Down Common, and there are several little pathways through the scrub and soon the Culm Davey Mast will be reached. Once here there is a lane to a pig farm and a road to the left, this is a much shorter walk and comes out to the same cross roads as the longer walk. From the mast the longer walk takes one down the dirt track on the right through forest and across moorland, again criss-crossed with many tracks, which are covered in gorse, heather and wortle berries. This moor is known as Culm Davy Hill. There are several different paths and again you should keep walking as near as possible towards the Monument. When the road is reached turn left towards the crossroads and then follow the signpost to Chard and Ilminster. Walk up there for a very short distance until there is a footpath through the trees, which leads up to the Monument.

Wellington Monument: Arthur Wellesley led the victory over the French at Talavera during the Spanish Peninsula War; for this he was ennobled and asked to choose a title. On September 4th 1809, he became Viscount Wellington of Wellington and Talavera. He chose Wellington for two reasons; it was the nearest to his family name, and although his family lived in Ireland, they originated from Somerset. He was given the Wellington estate in 1813. After further triumphs including Waterloo he became the first Duke of Wellington. He visited his estate here only once and that was in 1819. On the 20th October 1817, a meeting of wealthy businessmen decided to perpetuate the memory of the first Duke of Wellington, The Iron Duke, by building a Monument on a high piece of his estate. So now on this chosen steep escarpment, standing 175 feet high, it overlooks the town. The Duke died in 1852 and is buried in St. Paul's Cathedral. Work on the Monument was not completed until 1892, because the fund kept running out of money. The cannon at the side of the Monument was not used at Waterloo, but it was cast about the same time

Top: *Culmstock Beacon,* middle: *Popham Memorial inside Wellington Church, and the Wellington Monument,* bottom: *Wellington Church, showing how the gravestones are now around the edge to make easy work for the mowers.*

Wellington Church: empty niche which housed a statue before the Reformation.

in Scotland. The monument is now floodlit each evening and so can be seen for miles by day and night, it was designed in the shape of a bayonet by a Barnstaple man, Thomas Lee, and funded by subscription. It was supposed to have a statue of the Duke on the top but because the funds ran out it was left as seen today. The energetic can climb up the inside, there is a notice by the Monument stating where the key can be obtained. In 1989, considerable restoration of the Monument was carried out costing £150,000. More than forty tons of grouting was used. The woodland and point on which the Monument sits is now owned by the National Trust. 12½ acres have been owned by them since 1933, in 1954 another 54 acres were acquired, finally in 1966 a further 8 acres were leased from the Wellington estate. There is a lovely tangle of footpaths running around the Monument through the magnificent trees. Look especially here for some ancient trees which were coppiced a few centuries ago and now have several trunks coming from one root.

The meadows below the Monument are now managed as a Nature Reserve by the Somerset Trust for Nature Conservation. In these fields alone there is estimated to be 140 species of plants and wild flowers and among them the Common Spotted Orchid, Cats Ear, Wig-wam grass, Meadow Sweet and Foxgloves. There are over one thousand species of insects forming a continual supply throughout the year which in turn feed the many bird species. The surrounding trees are covered in lichen giving proof that the air in this region is truly unpolluted. These meadows have not been managed by intensive farming.

Whilst I was up here a group of horse riders came along. How wonderful to be up here on the bridle paths, walking, or whatever a horse does, through the trees. I wondered where they came from.

Heazle Farm: just a short way from the Monument, first turning left from the obelisk then taking the second turning right (signposted Clayhidon), Heazle Farm can be found, a horse-riding centre from which one can be taken around some of the most beautiful areas of bridle paths there are.

Hill Farm: back to the ridge road and still on the right hand side one soon comes to the next turning which is signposted Hill Farm. For the last four years deer have been bred here especially for venison which is fast becoming a popular and more common dish. Mr Graeme Wallace, the owner has introduced these animals to footballs, and they play quite happily. These are inquisitive and slightly aggressive beasts and they used to take their frustration out on each other, now they take it out on the ball. Sometimes they used to injure one another quite badly but now the deer are fully fit and keep on growing. As its name suggests the farm is situated on the top of the hills and this is highly suitable for these beasts who always choose the higher slopes when living in the wild.

Quarts Moor:
again take the left turning as you leave the Monument, this woodland will be found on the left. Owned by the National Trust (Eastern Boundary Line), it overlooks the Vale of Taunton Deane. This small isolated wood is surrounded by a road on all four sides but it is interlaced with woodland walks. It is ideal for walking dogs and for children and in quiet times it is even interesting for bird watchers. Going up the road from Ford Street (the road runs through the middle of this coppice), enter this wood on a footpath on its right hand side and there will be found a small cottage, with a veranda on three sides. In the 1800's an old lady lived nearby in what is now a ruin but she died of typhus. The National Trust now own it and use it, but it has a notice on it warning of danger because it is made mainly of asbestos. Back to the Monument.

Ford Street:
By the Monument there is a footpath marked "Wellington 2 miles". I followed this path, but then broke off to visit the hamlet of Ford Street. As mentioned in the Introduction, Ford Street was named probably by the Saxons who changed the crude high ridge track for man and beast into a highway, and this must have been where the road came down off the high ridge. The Romans went through this area but never settled. Nearly into Ford Street I found a large house called Briscoe. Built in 1706, the ceilings are very high, but it is not certain for whom it was built. The front rooms and door were built later, when it was turned into a gentleman's residence.

Wellington:
Back to the footpath mentioned above. Once in Wellington town, where today there is a population of about 13,000, there is quite a lot to explore, more than meets the eye at first glance. The first Charter of the town was signed by Edward the Elder, in 904 AD. Five years later the Manor of Wellington was given to the Bishop of Wells. There are several Georgian houses.

The Museum and Tourist Information Office at 35 Fore Street houses some interesting artifacts, and itself was once a 17th century posting house. Visiting it is free and one can read here how supplies of leeches were delivered to Wellington by train for T. E. Hooker the Chemist. Also found there is a history of the Dukes of Wellington, to the present day.

In 1600 the prison stood inside the Market House; when the Market House was demolished in 1822, the prison was moved to the site of the present Town Hall, which was built in 1833. Being housed in the prison was so diabolical that it was given the name of "Little Ease".

Wellington was once the main boom town when the textile industry was at its peak, from the 17th century and onwards. The Fox brothers built mills which were the main source of employment. When the textile trade declined the town took on various other industries and is now well known for its mattresses, bricks, and aerosol cans (in fact the first aerosol ever made was produced here). Because of the hole in the ozone layer aerosol cans are now having to be C.C.F. free. The Park in Courtland Road was donated by the Fox family.

There was a Railway Station here which closed under Dr. Beechings axe on October 5th 1964. The Salvation Army have a citadel in the town. The Gothic Congregational Chapel was opened in 1861 and the Baptist Chapel in South Street was opened in 1833 and enlarged in 1877. There is a United Reform Church in Fore Street and a Roman Catholic St John Fisher's Church in Mantle Street.

In 1873 a Fire Service was established under the jurisdiction of the Local Board, it had a captain, twelve men and two engines. Before this time fire services were run by insurance companies, who would fix an iron emblem to the exterior wall of the house insured. Fire engines would then only go to the people who were insured by the company concerned. Occasionally one of these iron fire marks can still be found.

There is an excellent Sports Centre complex which was opened on the 22nd September 1973 by Dr. Roger Bannister C.B.E. where one can swim, play badminton or even learn to ski.

Many famous people have lived in this town, but one of the most controversial was Sir John Popham 1533–1607. He was born at Huntworth and educated at Balliol College Oxford. He married Amy Adams in 1550 and he was twenty-three when his father died leaving him many estates. He became M.P. for Bristol, Speaker of the House of Commons, Lord Chief Justice, Solicitor and Attorney General. He was involved in the trials of Mary Queen of Scots and the Babington conspirators, Sir Walter Raleigh, Robert Campion, the Earl of Essex and the Gunpowder plotters. He sent word to Lord Burghley warning of the approach of the Armada. One of his trials caused much publicity. A man known as Wild William Darell had a problem with a young girl when she became pregnant and was unmarried. When the baby was due, he paid a midwife a large amount of money to deliver the child and keep silent. The midwife was blindfolded so that she would not see where she was being taken. As the baby was born Darell grabbed it from her and threw it onto a blazing fire. The sickened and frightened midwife slowly cleaned up her equipment and as she did so she cut a remnant from the curtains. She was blindfolded again and as she went out she counted the stairs. The following day she reported these happenings to the authorities. The house was identified and Wild William was brought to trial, but he paid off Judge Popham by giving him

16

Littlecote Manor. This bribe saved his life but losing the Manor hurt very much and so consequently he put a curse on the Popham family, so that there would never be another male heir. The curse proved false.

The story may or may not be true as Darrell was a friend of the Pophams and he himself had no heirs.

The Pophams became great landowners in this area, as will be seen when moving on to other villages. A hospital for six poor men and women and six aged men and women was endowed by Sir John Popham in 1606. It was very beneficial to the town and was rebuilt in 1833.

John Popham also had a wealthy friend called Peter Blundell, who founded nearby Blundells School in Tiverton. Popham was his chief executor. Popham was also chairman of the first committee ever formed to colonise an area of North America (see Richard Treat, Amberd House).

Another of Taunton's ex M.P.s, Sir Edward du Cann, made his home in the 15th century Cothay Manor, to the west of Wellington, which was built by the Bluets. The Bluets also built Greenham Manor.

There is a stone in Wellington called a cock-crow stone, which is supposed to cover buried treasure; legend has it that anyone happening to be there when the right cock is crowing could move the stone and get the gold. There is a similar stone at Culm Davy.

Littlecote: Three miles from Hungerford in Wiltshire can be found Chilton Foliat and this is the house for anyone wishing to hear more about William Darell. It is open to the public at specified times, and is said to be haunted by the Hounds of Hell which chase William on moonlit nights. There are also Roman remains to be seen on the estate. William came to his end when he broke his neck jumping his horse over a stile.

The Church of St John The Baptist: there was actually a church on this site in Saxon times but the present building is 14th century. The beautiful red sandstone tower and building stands on the east side of this busy little town. Either side of the tower door are empty niches, where statues were once situated before the Reformation. It will be noticed that the gravestones have been placed around the edge of the churchyard, to make easy work for the grass cutters. Inside is Sir John Popham's magnificent alabaster tomb which commemorates his death in 1607 at the age of 72. This tomb in the north aisle is very colourful and is supported by black pillars. John Popham, dressed in red robes and a black cap, has all his family around him. His only son Francis married Ann Dudley and they are the pair on the east end of the tomb. John also had six daughters and they are on the southside with their maids. On the north side can be seen Francis's children, five sons and eight daughters. John Popham is not actually buried in this tomb as his body was never found after he drowned,

so the effigy of him here is only a memorial. In his time John Popham was disliked by many people who would have preferred to have seen him in hell; consequently one of the most famous Blackdown ghost stories is based around him. It goes as follows:—

> One day he was out hunting between the Monument Hill (remember the Monument was not built at this time) and Wilscombe Bottom, when his horse stumbled and threw him into a deep pond. It was bottomless and so he went down to hell. His devastated wife prayed and prayed and gradually he started coming back, now each year on New Year's Eve at midnight, he advances one cock stride more towards Wellington Church.

Sir John Popham's house was taken and garrisoned for Parliament sometime after 1640 by Colonel Bovet. Sir Richard Grenville then attacked and destroyed the house on behalf of the Royalists. It is interesting to read the account of this war in Daphne du Maurier's book *The King's General*.

The ceremony of chasing out the devil, or Lent Crocking, always took place at this church on Midsummer Day. The dates that these old rituals took place varied from village to village and so did the ceremony. In Wellington people used to encircle the church and then dance for a certain length of time.

There is an unusual piscina here, held up by four stone heads, a king, a monk, a lady and a monkey. The pulpit sits on the vaulting of a 15th century screen.

John Robert Toms was the organist here for over fifty years. His father was a worker in stained glass and is responsible for many windows around the Wellington area (see West Buckland church). His son James Kelway Toms was famous for making violin and cello strings. He died in 1954. The organ is situated at the rear of the church.

This church chancel was restored in 1848 and when pulling down the old one the workers found more reredos smashed to pieces; all the faces were missing or disfigured. This would have been done at the Reformation (the Puritans believed it was wrong to have elaborate decorations) and the broken pieces probably hidden. The whole thing when it was in position would have been richly painted and gilded. It dates back to about 1380. It can now be seen pieced together again in Taunton Museum. There are two galleries at the rear of the church, one in the north aisle and one in the south.

The first recorded priest here was Stephen de Tornaco, Priest in Charge, 1215 AD.

The font has an elaborate cover, a lovely baptismal candle stands at its side, this is lit at every christening. There are beautiful hamstone piers in the nave.

With the success and prosperity of the Middle Ages and again in the Victorian era, most churches were either restored or rebuilt at these times and only fragments of Norman Architecture remain.

The wooden flooring caused concern in the 1980's when the main centre block of the nave and the north aisle was found to be rotten. About twenty pews had to be roped off when two people fell through the floor. The wooden floor was replaced by paving slabs and the removed pews were replaced with good quality chairs.

In January 1990 a hurricane of unusual force in this country caused several thousand pounds worth of damage when a pinnacle fell from the tower onto the main roof. It made a square meter hole in the lead. One piece bounced onto the lower roof and broke off one of the castellations.

I hear some lovely stories when visiting The Blackdown churches. The one I heard here was about the robin. Did you know that the robin used to be brown and white? One day a robin flew by as Christ was hanging on the cross, it felt very sorry for him as he was asking for a drink. The robin immediately carried a few drops of water in its beak to moisten the Saviour's lips, in doing so its breast became covered in blood. Since that day all robins have had red breasts.

Roman and medieval glass was placed when liquid into trays to set. Because it didn't run in evenly, it was smoothed with an instrument like a pallet knife, which made it thick and not always clear to see through.

In the 18th century glass makers started spinning the glass. A long pole would be held by the glass maker with the liquid glass on the end, this gradually grew bigger and thinner as it spun, like a big glass plate. When it cooled it was a lot clearer. The middle where the pole joined the glass was called the bull's eye. Squares would be marked on the plate and cut accordingly. The bull's eye in the middle would either be thrown away or sold cheaply to the very poor. Today the bull's eyes are very popular and although glass is no longer spun, but cooled in sheets on liquid tin, the bull's eyes are specially made and quite expensive. Coloured glass was first used in the 7th century. By 1000 A.D. stained glass was being set into lead and made into pictures. In the beginning very little blue was used, browns and yellows were easier. Very few people could read then, and by the 12th century the coloured glass windows in churches were looked upon as the library, as they told a story. They were iconographic, religious story books.

There was much destruction with the Dissolution, Reformation and by the Puritans in the 16th and 17th centuries, so almost all the medieval glass was lost; only small portions remain. In some churches it will be seen in fragments which have been found and put back into certain windows. If I find any on The Blackdowns I will point it out.

19

Glass matures with age as it gets patina on the outside which mellows the colours and this cannot be scrubbed off. When it gets very bad it has to be replaced. These lovely windows bathe church interiors in light and colour and give the cold stone churches a warm feeling, even on a cold dull day.

Webber's Grave: as I mentioned in the introduction, suicides were always buried at cross roads in the very early days, as they were not allowed in consecrated ground. In Wellington a lawyer called Webber continually cheated his clients and when he was inevitably found out, he committed suicide. He was duly interred at a cross road, with a stake through his heart to prevent his spirit walking, as was the custom. The stake could only be made of certain wood and that one made of elder was no good. That cross road still holds stories of a walking ghost which is occasionally seen, and therefore it became known as Webber's Grave.

Sampford Arundel: This little village surrounds the beautiful old church, but its boundary stretches down as far as the Beam Bridge and the main A.38 road. John Collinson said in 1791 that this village was situated three miles west of Wellington in the turnpike road to Tiverton and Exeter. Here once upon a time there was a sandy ford across the stream and it is from there that the village got its name. The Manor of Sampford Arundel was given to Roger Arundel by William the Conqueror. Roger Arundel was one of the main planners of the invasion of England.

The small river running from The Blackdowns turned a grist mill and then ran on into the Tone at Wellington.

A School Board of five members was formed in 1875. At Sampford Moor a Baptist Chapel was erected in 1871 seating eighty people.

Broadleigh Court on the west side of the parish has an ancient well which is mentioned in the Domesday book.

The Church of The Holy Cross: This 13th century church which was restored in the 15th century has a feeling of great age about it: the floor is very uneven and is made up of various flagstones and memorial stones, some long worn down and commemorating several different generations. The first recorded vicar was Robert Howel in 1324.

Before flagstones were used on church floors, rushes were always laid to create a pleasant smell, they collected all the unpleasant leavings of both men and animals, which were allowed in church at that time. It was an accepted practice for men to spit, in fact it was taken as a sign of masculinity. The rushes had to be changed regularly. Flagstones came into being in about the 15th century, when many churches were being rebuilt, especially in this area where the wool trade was flourishing. There had been a large acacia tree in the churchyard which was cut down in 1923, now part of its trunk is in the church with a brass plaque on it. Acacia trees were a novelty in this country in the time of Queen Elizabeth I, so I suspect that that is about the time when this one was planted.

The beautiful window over the altar, the east window, was erected to the memory of Edward Houlditch who died in 1836. He was a former fellow and bursar of Magdalen College, Oxford.

There was no one about to give me any information and there were no booklets or guides on sale. The tower had just been re-pointed. One of the children of the village had written the following prayer which I thought was worth including.

> Lord make me an instrument of thy peace,
> Where there is hatred, let me sow love,
> Where there is injury, pardon,
> Where there is doubt, faith,
> Where there is sadness, joy.

Sampford Arundel's little church is very homely and it was especially nice to see the local children taking such an active part. There was a large poster when I visited called "Everyone belongs in God's family" and the children had cut pictures out of magazines of various nationalities and had pasted them all on the poster.

Reading these children's bits and pieces reminded me of a story I was told by a teacher on my travels. It was the usual annual nativity play and one small spoilt little boy was determined to be Joseph; the teacher was equally determined that he wouldn't be. In the end he reluctantly accepted the role of innkeeper. On the actual night of the performance, with all the proud parents present, Joseph and Mary finally knocked on the inn door,

"Is there any room in the inn?" Joseph asked.

"Yes, plenty, come on in," replied the innkeeper.

In the north wall is a 13th century carving showing a hand holding a heart; the niche behind this was probably used for a heart burial.

There is also a marble memorial to Christopher Baker, who was High Sheriff of the county in 1724, it is dated 1729. There are many brasses commemorating young men who died at war.

Also some sisters and a brother gave a window in memory of two of their brothers who died at Gallipoli, this is worth looking at.

The fifth bell in the tower is inscribed,

> I sound to bid the sick repent,
> In hope of life when breath is spent.

The bell was used as the "passing bell" and is dated 1668.

The register dates from 1695.

Candlemas on February 2nd was an important date in the church calendar of the Middle Ages, especially in a farming area such as this. It is the Feast of the Purification of the Virgin Mary. It was important to these medieval farmers, villeins, because it signified the time to plant the crops, peas, corn, etc.

Reporting on these old churches reminded me of the reason for altar rails. They were put in front of the altar originally to stop the animals, which were allowed in church in the middle ages, urinating on the high altar. Also at this time there were no pews in church except for a few benches around the walls, everyone stood. These benches were for old people and children, hence the saying "weakest to the wall".

White Ball and Sampford Moor: These two hamlets belong to

Sampford Arundel. Here you will find the famous White Ball Bank, which is the steepest incline of any railway line in England. The line reaches its highest point in White Ball tunnel, which is one mile long. Over one hundred years ago this tunnel was dug into The Blackdown Hills completely by hand and the boast of the men was that they entered in Devon and came out in Somerset, or vice versa.

Because of the steepness of this piece of line, bankers (spare engines) were kept in a siding at Wellington to assist the passing engine over this section. This same section, because of its gradient, was also the stretch of line used to obtain the fastest time by a steam train in Britain.

I found that one can't go anywhere on the Hills without hearing something about one of the most famous eras of our history, that of the Monmouth rebellion. Two stories I heard in the Wellington area were

> On the 14th May 1685, two men were drinking in one of the taverns near Wellington. One of them was William Way of Combe St. Nicholas, the other was Mr Cross, the County Coroner. Cross was really fed up and Way, who was under the influence of drink, was very optimistic about the future saying that the Duke of Monmouth would be here by the end of the month and then all would be well. The secret was out; Cross passed it on to the Reverend Axe who was a Steward at Orchard House and he passed it on to William Portman in London.

The second story was about a Mr Sealey:

> One day, riding his horse from Exeter to Taunton, via The Blackdown Hills, he met a farmer on a grey mare. The farmer persuaded him to stay the night in a nearby lodging house.

When the inn came into sight, surrounded by rough ground, the farmer suddenly disappeared. Several men and women all carrying spears, then gathered around Mr Sealey, grabbed him and led his horse away, it was never seen again. The crowd kept lunging at him and he retaliated with his sword but it kept going straight through these shadowlike people. When daylight finally came the people disappeared and the inn was empty and abandoned. On relating his story later, he was told the innkeeper had been a supporter of Monmouth and had eventually been hanged from his own inn sign. The plot of waste land, where he had been held by the crowd, was a mass grave for the Rebels.

I couldn't find out exactly where this was supposed to be.

Culm Davey: This village is recorded in the Domesday Book and in 1133 AD, Sir William Widworth held this moor and valley. He gave it to his son David during the reign of Henry II and so it became known as David's Valley or Culm Davey.

The only part of the old Manor House which remains is the Chapel, known as Culm Davey Chapel.

King George VI and Queen Elizabeth, the Queen Mother, passed through here in 1942 on their way to inspect bomb damage at Exeter.

Whitehall: The linen fold panels in the chapel were erected by Mr Bowerman, a descendant of the Bowermans of Whitestone house, Whitehall. The house still stands and is now a farm house giving its name to this hamlet – Whitehall. There was also once a grist mill here. The Bowermans moved to Holcombe Rogus.

Hemyock: In one of the lovely little combes lies the village of Hemyock and here we are actually in Devon. The name of this village comes from the Saxon words Ham, meaning enclosure and Ock the name for Oak. There is a colourful green and yellow monument with pump in Hemyock village square, it reads as follows:

> In commemoration of the Glorious reign of
>   Victoria
> The coronation of Edward VII and
> the Restoration of peace in South Africa 1902
> Fear God and Honour the King.

When William the Conqueror arrived in England, he built many castles, one being here in the demesne of Hemyock; it was given to the Hidon family (de Hydones) from Clayhidon. In 1292 the Castle passed to the Dinham family by way of marriage (Dynehams) and then to the Asthorpes, when Sir Oliver Dyneham's daughter, Margaret, married Sir William Asthorpe. This castle was more of a Manor House and in November 1380 Richard II permitted William Asthorpe and his wife Margaret to fortify and crenellate with battlements their Manor House with a wall of flint and stone. Crenellation was the furnishing of the upper part of the parapet of a castle wall with battlements (openings for shooting through). This made Castles almost impregnable. From King John's reign onwards a royal "Licence to Crenellate" was needed and only families who obtained some honour or similar award could have this granted.

In the Civil War in 1643, John Popham, who then owned it, had it garrisoned for the Parliamentarians. After the Restoration in 1660, Lord Poulett for King Charles II had the Castle almost destroyed, as it had served as a prison for the Royalists. This was when all the walls and turrets disappeared except what can be seen today, but the Manor House remained. Later the estate was divided and the part containing the Castle came into the hands of John Graves Simcoe (Walford Chapel) first Lieutenant Governor of Upper Canada in 1791. The grounds are now open to the public from April to September.

The plague of 1646 caused 57 deaths, which would have been quite horrific in a community as small as this one. There is a Wesleyan Chapel which was built in 1838, a Baptist Chapel built in 1865, and a Roman Catholic Church built in 1938.

The main industry here, and the only one of its like in the hills, is the Culm Valley Dairy Company with its fine tradition of butter making. ("St Ivel Gold"), which celebrated its centenary in June 1986.

The Culm Valley Railway opened in 1876 with a station at Millhayes and ran here from Tiverton Junction. In 1886 a siding was opened to the milk factory. The line ceased to carry passengers in 1963, another of Dr Beeching's cuts, and the last train which ran on the 31st October 1975, was a special train, as only goods trains had run since September 1963. The milk factory at Hemyock had provided much of the revenue for this line.

The War Memorial to the Great War was unveiled in 1920 and stands on the site of Church House, which was demolished in 1886. Here two rivers run into the Culm, the Bolham runs into the Madford near Jewell Farm and the Madford runs into the Culm at Millhayes. There is a Tennis Club and a thriving Bowling Club which welcomes adults of all ages. The Star Inn, previously the Star of Bethlehem, one of the two main public houses in the town for many years, was burnt to the ground and the site is now a car park. The other public house was the Catherine Wheel, which then became the Cartwheel, then Railway Inn, it is now again the Catherine Wheel.

In 1063, the Order of Knights of St Catherine was founded. This was an organisation of men specially committed to protect pilgrims travelling to the Holy Land. They wore white surcoats; and on each was a wheel with spikes sticking out and across the wheel was a bloodstained sword. (Hence the Catherine Wheel). The name has been adopted by several inns across the country since medieval times.

When an invasion of England was anticipated in 1798, Simcoe was appointed Commander of all the military forces in the South West. During this period plans were drawn up for the evacuation of Hemyock, which fortunately were never put into effect.

St Mary's Church:
The first mention of this church is in 1267 but there were previous places of worship on this site. The Hydones, who were the Lords of the Manor, were the Rectors between 1267 and 1283. Second sons of noble families were expected to become clergy, so I suspect that that was the situation here. A shorter outer south aisle was constructed in 1330.

The church was rebuilt in 1847. The Norman tower is very low, because the owners of the Castle did not want the church to overshadow their building.

There are six bells in the tower, the last one cast in 1860. Three names appear on this bell – Francis John Kitson, Rector; James Bowerman and William Farrant, Church Wardens, together with the following inscription:

> I to the Church the living call
> and to the grave do summon all.

The font is Norman and the cover is a replica of the one in Exeter Cathedral. In the 14th century Margaret Dynham's husband founded a chantry dedicated to St. Catherine (see The Catherine Wheel). There is a piscina in the south wall. The organ was originally in Pitminster Church. The east window has the Crucifixion in one of the side lights, which is most unusual. The present cemetery is across the road from the church.

Simcoe's son, the Rev. Henry Addington Simcoe, preached the first sermon in this church after the rebuilding in 1847.

Culmstock:
This was another important station for the Culm Valley Railway, and I was told that in its time the line was very slow but very friendly. It was often known for the driver to stop the train so that he and

the guard could get out and pick a swede or a cabbage from an adjacent field.

The river Culm runs through this village on its winding way around some lovely woodland and countryside from its source at Culmhead.

R.D. Blackmore, who wrote Lorna Doone, was brought up in Culmstock, his father, John, was a curate here. His mother died of typhus when he was a baby when they lived in Berkshire but his father moved to Culmstock after her death. Richard was then brought up by his stepmother.

On the hill opposite the church is Culmstock Baptist Chapel (Prescott Mission Hall). A Museum at Pitt Farm exhibits horse drawn machinery, tractors, cars and many other items. There are two public houses one called the Ilminster Stage, coming from the time when the stage coach from Exeter to Ilminster passed through and the other is the Culm Valley Inn.

Another of the inhabitants here was Fred Temple, who became Archbishop of Canterbury.

All Saints' Church, Culmstock: The first thing noticed is the tree growing out of the tower. This is a Yew tree which has been there for about 200 years. The church dates from the fourteenth century, but there was a church on this site in Saxon times. Saxon remains were found when the Hagioscope was opened up.

The Hagioscope is a slit like opening, popularly known as the squint, in the wall between the aisle chapel and the chancel, through which a chantry priest officiating at a side altar could see the ceremony at the high altar.

There is a plaque over the door in the porch which reads:

This is none other than the house of God,
and this is the gate of heaven.

The window in the north aisle and also a brass plaque state that Frederick Temple was a Sunday School Teacher at Culmstock, who became headmaster of Rugby, Bishop of Exeter in 1869, Bishop of London in 1885 and Archbishop of Canterbury in 1896. He died in 1902. His son also became Archbishop of Canterbury in 1942, but died in 1944.

Also in the north aisle is the greatest treasure of the church, a cope, and the only one I found on the Hills. This 500 year old embroidery depicts saints, apostles and martyrs surrounding the Virgin Mary. Christ in Majesty is on the cowl. It is in a case with curtains to protect it from the light. It is thought that this work was hidden when Henry VIII's Officers destroyed all the elaborate church furnishings throughout the country. The work has been dated to the end of the 15th century.

A cope is a semi-circular ecclesiastical vestment worn by clergy at services, when the chasuble, or outer garment, is not used. In the Middle Ages it was used by monks on festive occasions.

The font cover was made by Mr Bowerman of Holcombe Rogus, it is topped by a dove and it reads as follows:

> To the glory of God and in Memory of
> Tertius Poole, Vicar of this Parish.
>   1909–1929

One thing I thought unusual was that the nave runs through the middle of the church, the pews are double and the aisles run down the north and south by the walls.

A steeple once adorned the tower, but this was removed in 1776 and four weather vanes were erected on the pinnacles.

Uffculme: Uffculme Manor was part of the estate given to Walter de Douai by William the Conqueror, and from this evolved the Barony of Bampton. It passed to the Cogan family and they held it in 1368. Here we are talking about a barony being a group of Manors and not an hereditary peerage.

The 16th century Shambles, benches covered by a roof, still stands in the Market Square. Shambles were a collection of stalls used for the sale of meat produce in the market place. There are now only two examples of these left in the country, here and at Shepton Mallet. The famous street in York was once the market place for all the York butchers.

The wool industry was very evident here and in the 18th century Uffculme serge was being exported to the Netherlands. Coldharbour Mill is a working Musuem run by water wheel and steam engines. One can visit the weavers room to see the spinning and weaving machinery, the dye rooms, craft workshops and the waterside restaurant by the fish ponds. This all once belonged to Fox Bros of Wellington. It is open from Easter to October on Wednesdays and Saturdays. The Old Brewery is now the Culm Valley Activity Centre.

In the present decade the inhabitants have been concerned because it was suggested that Hillhead Quarry be used as a tip for the dumping of unspecified difficult waste by Devon County Council. Residents of Uffculme fought the case, backed by The Blackdown Society, whose credibility stands well in this area.

St. Mary The Virgin: the tower and spire of this church were rebuilt in the 19th century. The pulpit of Flemish work is 18th century. The 15th century chancel screen is 67 feet long and has one of the earliest examples of fan vaulting.

Hemyock Church; Victoria Pump, Hemyock Centre, and Dunkeswell Areodrome.

The pulpit is 18th century. The church has a 15th century arcade on the south side and a 13th century arcade on the north.

At the end of the north aisle is the Walrond Chapel, which holds the elaborate and colourful tomb of Sir William and his wife. His son is also there and will be seen holding a skull in his hands, indicating that he died before his parents. The date on this memorial is 1663.

Hackpen Hill: At the moment local people are trying to get a golf course laid on this hill, but there is much opposition.

Simonsburrow: This is a small hamlet, still in Devon. The definition of a hamlet is a cluster of houses, without a church. The place name is first recorded in 1190 as 'Simundesbergha' meaning Sigemund's hill. There is supposed to be a crock of gold buried here. In the battle here between King Ina and the Dumonians in 710 AD, a large barrow was erected for the burial of some of the soldiers; the tumulus itself was destroyed in the 1880's when all the stones it contained were dug up and used for building.

Here today can be found the Ashculme Boarding Kennels—a good place to leave your pets when you go on holiday.

Dunkeswell: This lovely small village lies quiet and sleepy on the side of the hill some eight hundred feet above sea level. It takes its name from St. Patrick's well. The Madford Stream trundles through here and then flows into the Culm. Situated on the top of the hill overlooking the village is the Methodist Church surrounded by its own small cemetery. The village is most famous for its airport, also on the top of the hill, built by Wimpeys in 1941–42. It opened for the Americans in July 1943. For eighteen months the Americans flew PB4Y-1 Liberators from here to attack V1 and V2 launching sites in Germany. Joe Kennedy was stationed here and he was flying to Fersfield on July 30th, when the plane blew up and all the crew were killed. In March 1946 the airfield reverted to Care and Maintenance. By 1949 it was used as a Gliding Club. It was purchased by Westward Aviation Ltd, who leased it to Dunkeswell Aero Club in 1967. For anyone living in this part of the world and wanting to learn to fly, this is the place, skydiving and flying with the professionals. Joe Kennedy, was of course the elder brother of John F. Kennedy. There are many stories about him from the locals who remember him. One lady, Mrs Millie Sparks has his Air Force spoon with his number on it, 116667. He also gave her a handkerchief which is a replica of the American flag. He visited her many times when she lived at Glebe Farm in his off duty time and she says he was a real gentleman.

Further along the road past the airport will be found Bakers Skid

St. Nicholas Church, Dunkeswell: East window, with Sower and Reaper, and below American flag flies in the church.

30

School, the skid control and off road driving centre. Next door again is Dunkeswell Kart Racing Club.

At the moment plans are being made to run a road through the hills from Exeter to the airport, where a large leisure complex would be built. There is much opposition from the locals.

The Church of St Nicholas:

A church has stood on this site for several hundred years, but the present one was enlarged in 1817 and again in 1868. The oldest relic seems to be a Norman font with the possibility of it being even Saxon. The east window is in memory of a former church warden William Francis Farmer who died 6th October 1960. It depicts Christ in the centre with a sower on his right and a reaper on his left. The words are "While the earth remaineth, seed time and harvest shall not cease". How poignant in this decade with the ozone problem which was not even thought of in 1960.

On a tablet is found the memorial to the American naval personnel killed in operations from Dunkeswell airport, including of course Joe Patrick Kennedy, brother of John F. Kennedy (mentioned above). There is a book presented to the church along with the memorial organ and plaque by the Officers and Men of the United States Navy Fleet Air Wing 7, in memory of their 183 shipmates who gave their lives whilst serving at Dunkeswell airbase. The Stars and Stripes hang in the window beside the plaque and over the book. The book gives the names of these men and the next of kin, and a memorial service is held in their honour on the nearest Sunday to May 30th every year.

In the nave there are six corbels each one representing an angel. The angels portray the six daughters of General Simcoe of Walford, the figures were carved by Henry Ezard and have the initials of each daughter entwined in the stone.

General Simcoe's father fought with General Wolfe at Quebec in 1759. The south transept was paid for by Mrs Simcoe. The north transcept was built and paid for by public subscription.

Sheldon:

Sheldon a small village not far from Dunkeswell has another lovely little church called St James the Greater. It also has a brass rubbing centre and the village hall boasts about the best kept village.

St James The Greater:

There was a previous church on this site, and the oldest relic here again is the Norman font. The first Vicar was Martin de Schildon in 1327. A bell cast by Robert Norten of Exeter in 1430 sits on the floor. The church was restored in the 19th century, apart from the tower.

To the north of Dunkeswell lies Dunkeswell Abbey.

31

Dunkeswell Abbey:

It is recorded in the annals of Margam Abbey that on the 13th August 1201 AD, the Convent was assembled to select twelve monks who were to build an Abbey at 'Dunekeswille'. The founder Lord William Brewer was a distinguished man in his lifetime. He was Sheriff of Devon, a judge in the reign of Richard I, later becoming Sheriff of Cornwall, and then Sheriff of Dorset and Somerset. As a judge he helped to secure the release of Richard Coeur de Lion from captivity. He was also one of the Lords who signed the Magna Carta. He selected his burial place in the Abbey at Dunkeswell and died on the 24th November 1226 at the age of approximately 76.

By 1238 there was a Fulling Mill just a short distance from the Abbey, as the wool trade was now becoming a large and wealthy industry.

The Abbey held the rights to hold a weekly market at Broadhembury a village nearby.

Once established the Abbey acquired many gifts and bequests and so bought up many lands in Devon and Somerset. The lands were as far apart as Bridgwater in the east to Coleton (Collaton Raleigh) and Lincombe (Ilfracombe) in the west. These lands remained in the possession of the Abbey until dissolution in 1539. The Abbey then fell into ruin and some of the stones were used to build surrounding farms and cottages, until the mid 19th century, when the Simcoes used much of the remainder to build Holy Trinity Church. The remaining ruins of the Abbey are quite interesting, find the one last remaining corbel which depicts a former Abbot.

Holy Trinity Church:

This church stands upon the site of the original Conventual Church and was erected with stones from the Abbey ruins in 1842. It was consecrated on September 21st of that year. Around the altar can be found some 13th century tiles found in excavations on the site. A stone coffin with slabs of Purbeck stone stands in the north west corner. Its date is the 1200s and it contained the remains of a de Brewer, believed to be William, the founder and his wife. The Simcoes of Walford Cross had it put here as the de Brewers were found to be their ancestors. There is a story attached to this coffin. In 1852 a workman was walking along when he realised that the ground beneath him was hollow in the cleared area where the Abbey used to stand. He dug and found two stone coffins bearing the remains of a man, a woman and a child. The coffins were lifted out and the remains were buried in the south east corner of the churchyard. One of the coffins was placed over the grave to mark the spot. In 1914, this coffin was brought into the church where it is now on view.

The church is white inside with a red tiled floor. There is nothing much in the way of memorials, but lots of history about the Abbey to read and enjoy.

A transcribed copy of the Deed of Surrender can be seen in the church.

The Abbey was surrendered to the King's Commissioner and his men on the 14th February 1539.

Cistercian monks were reformed Benedictine Order founded at Citeaux in Burgundy in 1098. Whilst Benedictine Abbeys were usually in towns, the Cistercians settled in remote places. Their churches were plain and simple. They were not allowed to eat meat, fish or eggs. They wore habits of white undyed wool. At the Dissolution there were over one hundred Cistercian houses in England.

Hembury Hill:
Once this was a Neolithic village (3,000 BC). At that time it would have been more of an enclosure for keeping in animals, with flimsy huts for homes, from which men would go out hunting, rather than built for defensive purposes. It is believed that the site was abandoned and not occupied again until the Iron Age people. It would have then been used as a fort as well as a village, by the Celts. (Iron Age: 750 BC-40 AD).

This is the time of Christ and like David against Goliath they would have used slings and stones.

Later again the site was occupied by the Romans. They had a military camp at one end and this was excavated during the early 1980's, several of the finds are in Exeter Museum.

Excavations show that even in the early camps cultivation took place on the slopes of this hill, very much as it does today. This is one of the earliest known cultivated hill forts in the country. Early men grew wheat, barley and crab apples.

The site is 884 feet above sea level and it gives a wonderful view through 360 degrees to show how the combination of man and nature can work together and still benefit the countryside.

Walford Cross:
Walford Chapel. This family chapel on the former estate of Upper Canada's first Lieutenant Governor, John Graves Simcoe, was given to the people of Ontario by Sir Geoffrey Harmsworth, at a ceremony held on September 27th 1966. The Hon. James P. Robarts, Premier of Ontario accepted the deeds of the Chapel and grounds from Sir Geoffrey and the title to an essential right of way from Mr. A. G. Le Marchant. The gravestones, all cemented into the foot of the exterior walls of the chapel are interesting. John Graves Simcoe died six years after he had built the chapel, the gravestones for himself, his wife and several of his eleven children are all there (match up the girls' names with the initials on the corbals in Dunkeswell Church). Lieutenant General John Graves Simcoe was born in Cotterstock, Northamptonshire. He joined the army in 1770 and during the American Revolution he commanded the 1st American Regiment, The Queens Rangers. He became the First Lieutenant Governor of the newly formed Province of Upper Canada from

1791 to 1796; he founded his H.Q. and base at York, which is now Toronto. He lived in Walford Lodge but also owned Hemyock Castle at that time. In 1796 he returned to England unwell and he resigned his Commission in 1798, never to return to Canada again. He died on October 26th 1806 and is buried, as reported above, with most of his family at Walford Chapel.

Clayhidon:
Building was first mentioned here in 1086 in the Domesday Book. The village takes its name from the de Hydones family. There was then a mill with several Bordars (smallholders).

This mill mentioned in Domesday is now Mill Farm. The house has been restored many times so is of various ages, but it is still a thatched building. Down the road from the farm on the right hand side there is a plaque in the hedge to one of the men who lived here. It reads as follows:—

William Blackmore,
Land Surveyor,
Of Clayhidon Mills,
Was murdered on this spot
The 16th day of February 1853,
by George Sparks of this Parish
who was Executed at Exeter for
this horrid crime.

In 1539 and with the dissolution of the monasteries, most of this village belonged to Taunton Priory. Here there is a beautiful church. At the end of the churchyard is the Half Moon Inn, now an excellent place for refreshment. Part of this building is very old and it was once the Church House. When the church was having some restoration work done in 1536 the workmen stayed in this house, and it is believed to have been here since the 13th century. Eventually the Manor came into the hands of the Pophams.

In the 19th century a Devonshire preacher called George Brealey (sometimes spelt Brierley, many name spellings varied centuries ago) set up the Blackdown Hills Mission here in 1863 and opened a chapel in 1865. It worried him that the people of The Blackdowns were so wild and untamable. Eventually there were seven Mission chapels on the hills, today there are still four operating, one being here in Rosemary Lane. This is a completely independent religion. In 1888 George Brealey died. Rosemary Lane is a hamlet within Clayhidon parish.

Clayhidon School Room was built in 1824 and in 1870 a new school opened, when the Mission was being established, Walter Brealey, brother of John, was headmaster here. In 1980 a new School was built in Battle Street, and the old School is now the Parish Hall.

Clayhidon even had its own artist who lived here at Applehayes. His name was Robert Bevan and many of his paintings are of the Blackdowns. He was a leading member of the Camden Town Group, which flourished in London in the early part of this century.

Waterloo Farm: continuing along the road from Applehayes, at the gate of the next farmhouse I chanced to take a rest admiring and making a fuss of the four large dogs that bounded out to see me off. Their owner Mrs Trotter, cheerfully greeted me and on finding out my mission informed me that not one but two industries took place on this property.

First it was a sheep farm, and not an ordinary sheep farm, but one specialising in dairy products. The sheep, who wear bells around their necks, are milked twice daily and the milk is then made into yoghurts and cheeses. The yoghurt, which is very smooth, is sold in plain, rum and raisin and fudge flavours and is highly recommended. Among the people this farm supplies are Fortnum and Mason and the Castle Hotel in Taunton. Distributed far and wide this product is getting more popular with each consignment. Gestation period for sheep is 142-147 days and during the lambing season blue and white striped marquees are hired and these serve as maternity wings for the ewes. There are now over a hundred Friesland ewes on this farm. The milk itself is especially helpful to people with dietary problems and allergies to cows' milk. Commander Trotter who retired from the Royal Navy shortly after the Falklands conflict, took on this style of farming.

The second industry here is run solely by Mrs Trotter herself. It is called Dressing for Two. Mrs Trotter who is a professional embroiderer makes these exclusive maternity and large dresses entirely of her own design. They are not over expensive. Pregnant women often have difficulty in finding maternity dresses that are not "frumpy", especially for evening wear. I spent the next half-an-hour trying on some of these designs and wishing that my childbearing years were still with me. I did in fact end up buying one.

I had to smile to myself here because on walking straight up this lane from Waterloo Farm, one eventually comes out onto the ridge road again and on turning left one soon comes to Hill Farm. One minute there are sheep in the field with bells around their necks and a few minutes later there are deer playing football. One begins to believe in the myths, the magic and the fantasy of The Blackdowns.

St Andrew's Church: I walked into this church on a blisteringly hot day. I would have liked a drink, but the Half Moon was closed. The cool of the stone church was such a relief. There was no church guide to buy, so the following comments are mostly my own observations. The tower is

John Graves Simcoe, gravestone, at Walford Chapel and below York Inn, Churchinford.

stuccoed, which I thought spoilt an otherwise charming building. Look for the gargoyle on the tower which represents an evil spirit devouring a man. The church is mainly 14th century. There is a sun-dial over the porch which I became quite excited about, until I saw its date was 1721, as far as I could read, the figures being a bit indecipherable. The first vicar was Ralph de Hidon, 1274-75 and there is an effigy of him in the bottom of the south wall. When the church was rebuilt they did not take much care with this tomb, as it is half covered by the walls. The font is very old and is plain and made of golden ham stone. It has a carved cover, obviously made much later. The pews are all box pews. The reredos are wooden, very old, and have painted on them the Lords Prayer and The Catechism. Queenie May Lock was the organist for twenty years and when she died aged forty six in 1954 a new blower was installed to her memory. There is a piscina in the north wall. Six bells hang in the belfry and there is also a toll bell as one enters in the door under the belfry.

Stapley:

Stapley: This hamlet consists of the old Mill House which is about 150 years old and has been turned into an attractive private residence. The Mill Leat and part of the old water wheel can still be seen. It was working until about thirty-five years ago and at the end of its life it was used to run a generator, as the man who lived here was a mechanic.

Stapley (Manor) Farm is an old Tudor house. At one time Thomas Grey, Duke of Suffolk was Lord of the Manor and it is said that his daughter Lady Jane Grey stayed in this house. He connived with Edward Seymour to seat Jane on the throne and later he too was executed (see Hatch Court). There was once a large silk factory here and because of the lack of work in this area there was exploitation of cheap labour. The raw silk was brought from Taunton to be spun. The industry did not survive for very long.

The church at Churchstanton has a carved gallery which was specially built to accommodate the silk weavers of Stapley.

The silk industry was also carried on in Taunton, and here there is a road named after it: Silk Mills Road. The workers in Taunton made use of the water from the River Tone. The only silk factory left in the town today is James Pearsall's.

A popular bottled mineral water is produced at Stapley. The Blackdowns are the sources of three well-known rivers, the Yarty, the Otter and the Culm. The springs which feed these rivers produce a soft water which is pure and low in sodium content. Blackdown Spring Water is mostly sold in the west, but it is also supplied to a large airline so Blackdown water actually goes around the world.

37

Chapter Two
The Central Area

Luppitt: coming up from Dunkeswell one arrives at Luppitt Common, used for camping and walking. Crossing the road running through it one is led again into Luppitt village itself. Luppitt-by-the-Sea, I was told the locals call it because of the stream running through it, which once used to be a ford.

This village was mentioned in Domesday by way of Shapscombe, Greenway Farm and Mohuns Ottery.

During the 18th century this whole area was famous for its brandy smuggling. The village is built on a hill and from the bottom looking up the church tower looks like a fortified castle.

The public house is called the "Luppitt Arms" and opposite that is the village post office, otherwise this is a very small hillside community. At the entrance to the church carpark is a cattle grid and embedded in the hedge at the side is the Luppitt stone. It is thought that it was used to unload the tenor bell in 1550. Many villages have these stones and most call them devil stones (Churchstanton, West Buckland, Wellington, Staple Fitzpaine and Hatch).

Church of St Mary The Virgin: I was completely surprised at the size of this large church for such a small village. Though cruciform in shape, the cross section is in the middle, the chancel was also the biggest I found.

This 13th century church has a beautiful wagon roof made from locally obtained wood. The first Rector was Henry de Flemyng in 1247.

A wagon roof has closely set rafters with arched braces to give the appearance of the canvas tilt over a covered wagon. The roof can be panelled, plastered or left uncovered.

The next thing to catch my eye was the piscina, again the first of its kind that I had found. This one sits on a long column right in the corner of the chancel.

The font is an unusual square bowl which depicts on the east face the martyrdom of an early Christian saint by the local pagan chieftain, after betrayal by a friend. The west side is foliage. The north side is a conception of an amphisbaena, a double headed monster representing the evils of duplicity. The south face is a hunting scene.

A peal of Grandsire Doubles was rung here in 1960 to celebrate the birth of Prince Andrew, the Duke of York.

There was a bit of a museum touch here as a glass case displays valuable items which were left unused after restoration work, when the church was reseated and re-lit. Also, coming in the door on the left hand side, will be seen some old bosses. These are from the old flooring when a new ringer's floor had to be installed in 1924 because the old one was dangerous.

The organ was installed in 1904 and restored in 1954. It was worked by an electric blower from 1958 onwards.

In the porch is a notice which reads:

> The Incorporated Church Building Society granted £35 in 1869, £25 in 1886 and £20 in 1926, towards reseating this church upon condition that all the sittings are for the free use of the parishioners and that a collection annually shall be given to the Society.

The memorial here which left me thinking was to the Hutchins family, which is on the north wall and mentions the grandparents and the parents, but then at the bottom it says that the children, John dyed Oct 28th 1705 age 14 and Thomas his brother, dyed Feb 3rd 1711 at the same age.

Dumpdon Hill:
Walking out of Luppitt, keeping to the narrow lane, and following the signpost marked Wick, a place unheard of even by people living ten miles or so away, it will be seen that the road ahead is shown as a "No Through Road". Turn immediately to the left up a steep hill and this leads eventually to Dumpdon Hill, an old Iron Age hill fort and now the property of the National Trust, covering some 62 acres. (Iron Age: 750 BC - 40 AD). I was there in bluebell time, and I was also pleased to find a species of wild orchid, now nearly extinct. Climbing up through the bracken covered slopes to another flat area and then up again slightly to the very summit, one is rewarded with spectacular views on a clear day. On a 360 degree turn nothing blocks the view for miles even today, and it can easily be seen why the site was chosen as a hill fort by our early ancestors. The woodland which it overlooked would have been cleared and made into common grazing land for sheep, today it is a patchwork of small fields. Situated here is an O.S. Trig point, Bench Mark 1709, and immediately behind there is planted a small plantation of various trees. The planting was begun in January 1967 by J.C. Udale for the Honiton Rotary Club. Walking through this small wood and out on to the road on the other side leads one to the village of Beacon.

Beacon:
This is a very small hamlet but it has some lovely thatched properties. There once was a chapel which is dated 1859, but it is now a private residence.

39

Hartridge Common:
On the north side of Beacon there is another common, Hartridge. This has a tumulus. There are more magnificent views, and it is possible to walk its full length.

Upottery:
As the name suggests the River Otter runs through here on its way down to Ottermouth. This was a Saxon settlement, but at the time of the Conquest it came into the hands of Rouen Cathedral. In 1267 it was handed over to Exeter Cathedral. The Manor or Rawridge, of which Upottery is a part, was held by the Cheneys at the time of Edward I. (William Cheney of Poyntington).

It is a lovely little village with a ham stone cross in its centre, it once had a large coach house which is now turned into luxury flats. I had another lovely meal in its only pub "The Sidmouth Arms".

St Mary The Virgin Church:
In the opinion of a London architect who was consulted in 1875 this is a 12th century church, although it was rebuilt later. It is also known that there was a church on this site as early as 705 AD. The first known vicar was Robert de Charde in 1285. One of the oldest pieces is the piscina dated about 1250. The tower is 15th century. A clock was placed in the tower in 1793, one can read all about the mechanics of it on the left when entering under the tower. There is a Norman corbel table. The church was restored in 1875. One of the vicars, James Burnard, was gaoled in Hemyock Castle for refusing to use the Presbyterian Directory at the time of the Civil War.

Smeatharpe:
This hamlet, belonging to Upottery, high up on the hills, was once called Smith Harp. It is I suppose now best known for its stock car racing; trailers with battered cars can be seen going off into the hills at week ends, providing an exciting sport for those interested. This takes place on an old airfield which was purpose built for the Second World War. Now the only drone, thankfully, is from the enthusiastic microlite flyers, and on this same patch all the local H.G.V. Drivers get their first tuition and introduction to these big modern day dinosaurs. Again on the same area a Sunday Market is held, selling anything from a joint of beef to a white elephant. There is so much hidden away on the summit of the Hills.

Newhouse:
I found this small patch of houses with the Baptist Chapel sited in the centre. The church, as I was told by the Minister John Woolham, is an Independent Baptist Chapel and not associated with the Baptist Union Denomination. This came about because the parishioners disagreed with some statements made by a leading figure in the Denomination about important church doctrine. They still function in the same manner as when they were in the Denomination but they are now an

autonomous body. This church was founded in the year 1652 and was rebuilt in 1859.

Fishponds House:

retracing one's steps back from Smeatharpe on the way to Honiton there will soon be seen a signpost marked Fishponds House, pointing off to the right. This leads down a steep road and right at the bottom on the right hand side will be found the caravan and camping site of Fishponds House. This lovely complex is a real hideaway for holidaymakers who want to get away from the crowds. The Fishponds, made by the River Bolham running through, was the original fish farm belonging to the Cistercian Abbey of Dunkeswell (strange when remembering that Cistercians didn't eat fish). The ponds are fascinating with their wildlife and fish. There is a swimming pool where even casual passersby can enjoy a swim before a meal. Cream teas and all vegetables fresh, are only some of the things advertised by the owners. The grounds, untreated with chemicals and fertilisers, cover eighty acres and are a wildlife sanctuary with extensive badger sets, deer, wild ducks and rabbits. For holidaymakers actually camping on the site there are hot showers, toilets and electric razor points. The hot water is provided free and the lights are kept on all night in the toilets. Instruction will be given to windsurfers on request and boats and rafts may also be taken on to the large pond. Tennis, snooker, fishing and other activities are available and planning permission has just been granted for a 9 hole golf course.

Burnworthy:

clay pigeon shooting takes place here. I believe this is a much better hobby and target practice than shooting the birds. It takes place on two sites, one in an old disused quarry which cannot be seen from the main road, and which is part of Westcombe belonging to Nigel Hankey. The other site is some private land at Culmhead belonging to Burnworthy. There is opposition from locals who don't like the repetitive popping of the guns and an enquiry is being held with a view either to ban the clay pigeons or to muffle the sound.

Also here is the Combat Zone, run by Mr Phillips of Burnworthy Manor. War Games, people have fun firing biodegradable pellets at one another in this twenty five acres of woodland, is I imagine a great way of obtaining exercise and fresh air and much better than partaking in the real thing. Burnworthy Farm itself was here 600 years ago and its produce used to supply the Cistercian monks at Dunkeswell.

Churchinford:

I walked into Churchinford village and stood at its six cross centre. The thatched cottages, pub and shops are all obviously very old. I first took the road marked Moor Lane, towards Fairhouse Farm. Soon on the right hand side will be found Post Boys Cottage and Ostlers

41

Fishponds House.

Cottage, both two hundred and fifty years old. One can often find these two types of cottage next to each other, as the ostler used to look after the horse and see to its needs for the postboy, when he rode in with the mail. Continuing on this narrow undulating road past the Ford House Restaurant one soon arrives at Fairhouse Farm itself. This thatched property now has a preservation order on it. It is L shaped and the part facing one is 15/16th century, probably an old long house, as it slopes slightly and the byre would have been at the lowest end. This now joins the other part of the L which was added slightly later. The old remains of the Chapel of Ease have been rebuilt into a barn-garage and is by the entrance gate. The farm gets its name from the fact that the annual fair was always held here on St Paul's Day. The fair was started by the Tudenhams, holders of the Estate in the reign of Henry III. Further down the lane there is a stone bridge across the River Otter. This used to be the Ford, which is how the village got its name: the church by the ford. Over this bridge the lane becomes known as Knackers Lane, as the animals from the fair and the village were brought down here to be slaughtered. Down this lane I found some cowslips, (primula veris) identified by the leaves as belonging to the primula family, another flower which used to be numerous but these days takes some finding.

Back in the village there are some cottages and the York Inn which date from the 15th century. When renovations were being done to the pub a Priest's Chamber and a Cromwellian sword were found. A Cromwellian sword was also found in the Post Office.

Churchinford had no Police Station in 1914 but by 1919 one was established. The Police Force was established in 1829 by Sir Robert Peel. Before this time the only real kind of force was the Bow Street Runners. The County Police Act of 1839 enabled Justices to establish a paid Constabulary for the Somerset Force. 1856 to 1860 are now looked upon as the years of construction. Training and discipline were severe. Financial problems were the biggest bugbear for the hiring of an ever increasing force. Regrouping took place after the first World War and gradually each village got its own "bobby".

Again from Churchinford centre take the road to Hemyock, and one comes to a crossroad, with Woodbine Cottage on the left and Redlane on the right. Standing at this crossroad, just across the road on the opposite right hand corner a footpath starts; hidden away in the hedge and covered in ivy, the footpath is marked 'Churchstanton Church 1½ miles'. Here there is a well made strong stone ladder stile. I am always surprised by little things like this hidden away, found when walking, but never noticed and driven past in a car. This footpath leads into a field, and eventually comes to a track, which takes you down into Willands Farm and out on to the road nearly opposite Churchstanton School.

Churchstanton: There was a very large settlement here in ancient times but all that is now left are large blocks of stone. These stones were later called Devil Stones and were supposed to have mystical powers. Some youngsters going home one night dared the Devil to come out; this he did and followed them home, remaining outside their house until morning.

The Manor was in the hands of the Tudenhams in 1282 but eventually was another to come into the ownership of the Pophams. Thus it remained for over two hundred years, when it was sold to Mr Southwood.

This village was in Devon until 1896, when the boundaries were changed. This makes it the only parish in Somerset which is in the Diocese of Exeter.

The Church School was opened in 1850 and was within the grounds of the Parish Church. A School Board of five members was set up in 1875 and the school became a board school on February 22nd 1876. The present school was built in 1879 on this site at the cost of £900; it was for 130 children, both girls and boys. It was opened on October 20th 1879. According to Kelly's Directory, by 1906 there were six Managers on the Board.

In 1897 it was reported that there was a considerable amount of iron ore in the Parishes of Churchstanton and Otterford.

Returning to the track and footpath behind Willands Farm will take one on to Churchstanton Church.

St Peter and St Paul's Church, Churchstanton: A church existed on this site long before the Normans invaded our Island, but the earliest part of the present building is the chancel which is 13th century. This church seats 250 people. It has an elegant arcade dividing the nave and aisle. As with all churches, work was carried out for generations so each century left its mark. The more affluent society at the time, the grander the benefits were to the church. The entrance in the 14th century church was in the north wall, but this is now blocked up because in the 15th century a new door with golden ham stone was put in the west wall. The church displays several gargoyles and some have lead piping inserted through their mouths, which serves as a drainage system. There are also stocks in the churchyard.

Inside there are five nave arches and a wagon roof. There is a piscina in the south wall. The gallery was added in the 19th century to accommodate the silk workers of Stapley. No-one knows quite how old the font is, but it is believed to be Saxon. There is a memorial to a man who gave his life in the Great War, and in his memory there is a bed in Taunton Hospital for any silk worker from Churchstanton or Otterford who may need it. There are 14th century carved capitals and some 15th century window tracery. There are two Jacobean chairs in the chancel with the arms carved like snakes.

In 1660 Joshua North, a Tanner's son, became the Rector and was the first married man to do so. Another outstanding Rector was A.D. Taylor who was known as the "Radical Parson", he was a socialist and known for giving most of his money to the poor.

The register dates from 1662. After 1538 each Parish had to keep a register of baptism, marriages and burials; before this time it depended on the efficiency of the priest.

In the week when I walked this area, I picked up the magazine for Churchstanton, Buckland St Mary and Otterford Church and Village news. In it was this joke:—

"Who sits at the right hand of God?" the Sunday School teacher asked.

"Mrs God," a voice replied.

Next door to the Church is Churchstanton House which used to be the Old Rectory, but now another building called The Rectory stands next door again. There is a footpath between these two houses pointing to Redlane and Otterford.

Burnworthy, Biscombe, Redlane and Stapley are all hamlets belonging to this Parish.

Merland's Corner: at Merland's Corner near Churchstanton, there

was reputedly the home of a miser, his money all hidden way in his cottage. One day a big white dog arrived at the miser's house and although he made enquiries all around the area as to whom the dog belonged, he never found an owner. By this time he had become quite attached to the beast, who he named Merland. One day a gentleman arrived in Churchstanton and told all the locals that he was the hermit's brother. He stayed around and people saw him everyday but did not question where he was staying or for how long. Early one morning Harry Peck, one of the local farmers, was going off to milk his cows when he found a body lying at the side of the road. The big white dog was walking up and down growling and whimpering. The old hermit was dead, with wounds said to be more vicious than could be dealt by a man. When the villagers got to his cottage it was totally devastated; even the floor boards had been pulled up. Did someone hear about the miser's wealth and make a picking? If so why didn't the dog fight him off? Was it because the dog knew the murderer? Was it the brother? Neither the brother nor the dog were seen from that day, but there is sometimes seen at this bend in the road the ghost of a white dog with extremely large eyes. I hope the readers never see this, as it signifies a death in the family.

There is, always, another ghost story attached to this crossroads, this time concerning a white horse.

From Churchingford again, on the road towards Bishopswood, will be found a footpath at Royston House Farm, which leads across the fields into the woodland of Otterhead Estate.

45

Otterford: this parish is very widespread being mainly agricultural. The ancient name was Ford taken from the family who were tenants of the Manor under the Bishopric of Winchester.

Otterhead Estate: the river Otter rises just above the site of Otterhead House at Yalham Farm and soon surges, crystal clear, into the lakes and waterfall of this estate, which now belongs to the Wessex Water Authority. The estate at Otterhead stands 700 feet above sea level. It is in part leased by the Forestry Commission and by the Somerset Trust for Nature Conservation. Trout fishing is available, but only fly fishing from the banks is allowed and anglers have to be careful of the many visitors walking the lake footpath. The lakes are well stocked with rainbow trout and brown trout. Fly fishing permits can be obtained from the lodge.

In 1841 William Bleadon, a Taunton surgeon, designed and built the six-turreted Manor house (Otterhead House) in Tudor style, together with four cottages, and the lodge. It is on the site of Week Farm, an ancient farmhouse. The estate covered one hundred and fifty acres. In 1864 William died and the Otterhead Estate was bought by the Mellor family. Sir John Mellor was deputy Lieutenant for Somerset and was also a J.P. for Devon. Originally there were five lakes but only two remain. Otterhead House overlooked the top lake which is still there, at that time it was called the House Lake. The estate was sold in 1894 to Robert Lewis Lloyd and it was leased out in 1905. The house was last inhabited in 1937. All that remains today is the lodge, and over the bridge and up a path, can still be seen the corner stones of the old Manor House, also part of a walled yard, with the stable block and coach house. It was taken over by the Water Authority in 1939 and by 1947 the building was in such a state of dilapidation that Taunton Corporation decided to have it demolished because it was unsafe. The bottom lake is called Royston Lake and the remains of an old boat house can still be seen at the top of this lake, which is also the habitat of numerous wild birds. The estate had its own trout hatchery, its own acetylene plant, which provided gas for the house. The lawns and grass tennis court were grazed by a pony, who wore special shoes to not damage the turf. Big estates like this one were little self-sufficient communities. This one supported several children who all went to the local school, and there is a footpath from here across the fields by Otterford Church to the School house, which is mentioned later. The produce from this estate was sent by rail to London and sold in Covent Garden vegetable market. There is now a good car park and information board at the top of the drive by the lodge, placed there by the Fisheries and Recreation Officer. In the trees half way down this drive are the remains of the four cottages.

The River Otter meanders on through Ottery-St-Mary and finally emerges in the English Channel at Ottermouth.

I walked this footpath several times during the two years throughout the seasons, but my favourite time was bluebell time, the colour of the magnificent carpet under all the trees was spectacular and the scent intoxicating. Bluebells (endymion non-scriptus) are abundant in woodland and flower between April and June. In Elizabethan times, starch made from the bulbs of bluebells was used to stiffen the elaborate collars and ruffs. Now it is illegal to dig up bluebell bulbs.

There is a nature trail, well marked and needing no explanation; the footpath makes a steep descent from the car park and in the spring and early summer the rhododendrons on either side of this lane are beautiful – these together with the bluebells, honeysuckle, campions, snapdragons, marsh marigolds and many others are the reason for the notices which warn against picking wild flowers.

This is a paradise for conservationists and ornithologists, who love the variety of wildfowl here. I have to admit that I left the trail in the dark forest and wandered off in search of badgers, as I had heard there were some about. Sure enough I found a well used set, but I didn't see any badgers because, of course, they are nocturnal creatures.

St Leonard's Church, Otterford:
This small grey stone church with its squat tower, was built in the 13th century and repaired and enlarged in 1861 when the north aisle was added. It is hidden away but it is well worth making the effort to explore it. There was a church previously on this site as is the case with most churches. Over the porch is a sundial, with an inscription which reads "Our days on the earth are as a shadow". In the fourteenth-century and before, the priest would watch the sundial for the time of the service and then ring the bell to call all the parishioners. This was in the age when everyone had to attend church. Employers would whip their apprentices if they skipped church. There are many stories of the priest getting the time wrong because the sun was not shining and therefore the sundial did not work. These Mass Dials were always put on the south side of the church.

This Church sits between two rivers, the Yarty and the Otter. It is also half way between Exeter and Glastonbury, two very important places in the early years of Christianity and this church was a pilgrim church, run by two monks who lived in what is now Holman Clavel, for pilgrims on route.

The oldest artifacts seem to be an Elizabethan chalice and a Norman font. A piscina in the Chancel and a water stoop on the south side of the church are very old, but what fascinated me was the head of what appears to be a bishop on a corbel, but I couldn't find out who he was supposed to be.

The corbel of a former incumbent at St. Leonard's, Otterford and below *Higher Fyfett.*

48

There are brass memorials to the Combes family of Fyfett Court, one of them reads:

> Injurious death, thou hast now shown thy spite,
> And yet my dust shall see eternal light.

There are several memorials to the Willie family of Fyfett. They are dated from 1640 to 1702 with various spellings of their names. Remember also the fact that the old calendar was still in use and therefore New Year's Day was March 25th.

The church register dates from 1558 but is incomplete as apparently a local shop keeper, who was also a Church Warden, used parts of it for wrapping up his goods, round about 1810.

Outside in the churchyard there are two very old table tombs. One, dated 1629, is to Richard Willey of Fyfett and the one beside it is to his son Richard, dated 1666. The inscriptions are very hard to read but the tombs are about the oldest I have found so far on the Hills.

The church was repaired and enlarged in 1861.

John Boles died on the 2nd February 1769 and he left the sum of £50 to the Minister and Church Wardens, in trust, that they might every year teach six children from six poor families in the parish to read.

The Charity Commissioner's Reports from 1819-1837 were unable to trace any source of this trust since Sarah Willie had kept the School in 1784. In 1778 Otterford became a parish in its own right, before that time it had been attached to Angersleigh.

A new roof was put on in 1925. Alan James Grabham (1892-1961) was a churchwarden here and when he died his widow gave the outside Porch Doors as a memorial to him.

Part of the church farmhouse used to be the vicarage but a larger vicarage with a small school attached, was built in Bishopswood. When the school on Brown Down was built in 1882 this small school in Bishopswood was closed and then used as a Chapel of Ease to Otterford. All these buildings have now been sold off as private residences.

Back to the Church and farm and opposite the farm on the bend an unmarked footpath starts, and two fields away in the middle of the field is a pit called Marl Pit (old Marl pits like this one are common on the hills, as marl deposits have been found and quarried); this one was filled with trees and scrub and here we disturbed two young deer who went leaping off gracefully towards the copse.

Another footpath starts in the corner of a sharp bend in the road, just past St. Leonard's Church going towards Otterford Lakes. There is a footpath marker to Fyfett. It crosses fields to School Farm; just here on one side of the farm house by the main road, the B.3170, you will see the remains of two long Neolithic Barrows. These are two of the 'Robin Hood Butts' or 'Rues' and there are three more round ones along the road towards Bishopswood, which are clearly marked on the O.S. Map. They are ancient tumuli measuring about 60 feet in diameter and they are attributed to the bronze age (the bronze age began as early as 2,000 B.C.). Round barrows were common as burial chambers at this time. They were used later as butts for target practice for archers, taking the name Robin Hood, after the most famous archer of all.

As always there is a mythical story. It goes like this: two giants lived up here and they spent a lot of time throwing stones at each other. In 1818 some workman from Chard dug into one of the heaps and found a pile of flints.

There is another story (I have found that there are often several versions of these fanciful stories):

> One day an employer in the area set all his men digging away at the mounds to find the buried treasure. When they returned the following day there was no evidence of the previous day's excavations, and plants were growing again over the humps. The workmen, frightened, refused to dig any more, so the boss then started work himself, digging a large hole. Resuming after his lunch break, no hole could be seen. Local farmers also tried to use stones from these barrows, but mysteriously the stones always returned to the humps; the farmers concerned would then suffer some ill fortune.

Higher Fyfett Farm: once Fyfett Court was the home of the Willies and the Combes. It is a very beautiful old farmhouse which was built in 1677 and restored in 1861, even so there was a building on the site previously as Saxon remains can be seen in the west wall. At one stage of its history it was a thriving cheese factory, and much of the original equipment still remains. This is still a working farm run by the Sparks family.

Lower Fyfett Farm: this farm was once the outbuildings to Fyfett Court, then it became a farm but now it has been sold off and the buildings made into luxury flats and apartments.

Higher Whatley Farm: another old building on a working farm and above the front door is the following inscription:

> Let wisdom alone flourish and folly ever cease.

50

Walland Farm: once famous for its butter making, there are still men in the village who can remember the women that used to walk all the way into Taunton Market from here with large baskets on their arms, to sell the butter.

Abywood: there is a network of roads just above the Holman Clavel and on an unclassified road running parallel with the road to School House you will find Abywood Boarding Kennels, a Pussy Park of Distinction.

Holman Clavel Inn: a room in this building was once the school to which children from the Otterhead Estate would come, until 1882 when the School House was built further up the road. It was called the "Home" Inn, Clavel before 1875. Prior to that it was a coaching house where the monks used to stop on their way from Exeter to Glastonbury. It is 600 years old and there are still niches for holy water in this famous monks' resting place. It was later turned into a bailiff's cottage and then a poor-house, during which time a baby was born to a young girl there. It was a thatched building until the early twentieth century when the thatch was replaced by slates. The pub is owned by Otterford Parish Countil. The beam across the fireplace is a full holly beam. 'Holm' is a holly bough, 'Clavel' is a chimney beam, Holman means made of holly. It is said that the phenomenon of finding a piece of holly large enough to make a chimney beam, was reason enough to give this pub its name. The site of an old oven, now blocked up, can be seen.

The fireplace also houses a ghost called Charlie, whom all the locals will speak about. Charlie plays skittles, moves heavy furniture and even breaks glass, but there is never any debris left in evidence of these disturbances. The previous landlord spoke to locals about these happenings. The present landlord was standing by the bar and on being asked about Charlie, he said he had never seen or heard him and didn't really believe in ghosts, with that a dagger which hung on the wall, well secured with two large staples, fell off missing the landlord by about half an inch: he no longer denies Charlie's existence.

Charlie was a monk and was defrocked for doing something that monks are not allowed to do. One can imagine the shame and persecution of 600 years ago and so Charlie probably either took his own life or met a violent end at the hands of others.

The rafters in the roof are made from green untreated oak trees grown on The Blackdowns. The Holman Clavel has a restaurant and the food is highly recommended.

Now in 1991 with the Poll Tax, the Parish Council is urging locals to use the pub, which they own, and in so doing they will slightly reduce the Poll Tax in their Parish.

Holman Clavel and Angersleigh Church.

An annual Cattle Fair was held at the pub about 29th October, remains of the pound are still at the side. This was still in progress at the beginning of this century.

The field immediately opposite the pub was once the ancient village green for Otterford.

Straight up the road past the Holman Clavel are the School House, Meetings and North Pole Farm.

North Pole Farm: this is a working farm but here one can hire a bicycle and be supplied with a map, and once up here on the hill it is easy to ride the full length of the ridge road.

Meetings: this was once the home of two men who became sheep rustlers and were subsequently deported to Australia. Here in 1874 the building was purchased by the Blackdown Hills Mission (George Brealey) for £100, and it became Brown Down Chapel. This was a great sum of money in the 19th century and so he borrowed the money from a lady and paid it back at £4 per year. It was one of seven Mission Houses on the hills then. During the Second World War Brown Down Chapel was used as a rest room for soldiers and airmen. In 1980 it was sold again and is now a private residence called "Meetings".

School House and Six Gables: next door to Meetings, are the Old School House and Six Gables. In 1882 Mr Mellor from Otterhead Estate sold a corner of his field for ten shillings to a Board of Trustees of the Parish, who then built the Board School at a cost of £300. There was a clause in the deeds which stated that the School had to revert back to Mellor's descendents when it ceased to be a school. With the Education Act of 1902, the school became a National School and that clause was quashed by the Council. The School was called Bishopswood School but, like Bishopswood village, it is in the widespread parish of Otterford. It remained open until 1966 when it was sold for a private residence and is now called Six Gables, for obvious reasons. The house adjacent to it was the school mistress's house, and is now also a private residence called The Old School House. Over the front door of Six Gables there is a slit in the wall like an arrow slit, this was where the bell rope came through attached to an outside bell. Unfortunately the bell has at some time been removed. There is a well here and the water used to be pumped up into two large tanks in the roof. On The Old School House next door there is a thermometer-like instrument, which used to tell the level of the water in the tanks. When the tanks were low the children would have the duty of pumping to fill them up again. (From here along the main road past Robin Hoods Butts and on to the Devon Somerset border, is all known as Brown Down Common). There is a

footpath adjacent to these houses which goes across the fields once more to Otterford Church, but let us retrace our footsteps to the Holman Clavel.

The footpaths are beginning to knit together the small ancient communities of farmstead, school and church.

Holly Bush Caravan Park:
This caravan park situated down the road from the pub, and also named after the holly tree, is off the beaten track and therefore never overcrowded. It has all the necessary facilities including a shop, and is well worth a visit either to stay for a quiet few days in the Hills, or to rest overnight on the way deeper into the west country. It is an ideal base from which to look for the treasures of The Blackdowns. One may even be lucky enough to find some fossils as many have been found in the layer of greensand which was deposited on these hills about 70 million years ago.

Priors Park Wood:
across from the Holman Clavel there is a track which is a footpath and bridleway. It has a footpath marker saying "Blagdon 2½ miles". It is very marshy at all times of the year, so sensible footwear is a necessity. Near the top is a fork in the path and the right hand path takes you through to Feltham. The left hand path meanders down through Priors Park Wood, the scent down here, mainly from the coniferous trees, gives you the feeling of being free, far from habitation and work, a sweet foretaste of heaven. There is a great variety of trees in this wood, the broad leaf species being dominant. This walk finally comes out at Curdleigh Farm and then takes one up the lane to Blagdon village. I sat down on a log in the middle of this beautiful wood; the thickness of the tree trunks fascinates me. The sun was dappling down through the leaves and I was enjoying the utter serenity, when a fellow walker went by carrying a radio. The broadcaster was quoting one of President Bush's Senators as saying "We haven't got nuclear weapons just as a deterrent, if necessary we would press the button". I am not allowed to print here my feelings, at that moment. Since I started this walk and documentation, heavy machinery has gone into the top part of this wood to remove timber and undertake replanting. I am told this will take about twenty years.

Widcombe Bird Gardens:
again I visited in the spring and the sight of the azaleas and the rhodedendrons in this twenty acre park was well worth the entrance money, without seeing all the birds and animals. Incidentally, I say animals because there is almost everything here from llamas and deer to rabbits and rats. One can relax and wander around the lakes or just sit and watch it all go by.

Trickey Warren:
here is the home of Composite Signals, Government

Secrets. G.C.H.Q. employs many local people who commute mainly from Taunton and Wellington. It is erected on the summit of the Hills and known as Trickey Warren.

Around the outskirts of this secret base runs a footpath and wandering around the back it will be noticed that once this Radio Station was an aerodrome. It was used essentially as an emergency landing ground. During the Second World War it was a busy place. On April 20th 1944 there was a sudden influx when a Squadron led by Lieutenant Commander N.G. Buster Hallett, DSC RN flew in. This 24 Naval Fighter Wing had been specially formed for D. Day and was based here to work with 10 Group R.A.F. The Squadron flew more than four hundred sorties over France during the next few weeks, but did not encounter any enemy aircraft. In August 1946 Culmhead airfield was closed.

On Trickey Warren Farm there are some round barrows and on Glebe Farm there is an earthwork which forms a double circle. These can be reached via the footpath from Churchstanton Church.

Angersleigh: as I wandered through all these little villages, I saw all

around me the colourful hanging baskets, heard the mowers at work, smelt the freshly cut grass and admired the neat stone walls and weedless gardens. It was all so peaceful; was I really in the same world as war, atrocities and starvation? Begone strife. Let all mankind learn how to enjoy these simpler things in life. This is the smallest parish in the Ecclesiastical Parish in the Diocese of Bath and Wells of four hundred and twelve acres and with about fifty inhabitants. A tributary of the River Tone runs through here. Standing on the church steps, looking towards The Blackdown Hills, one faces the original tithe barn; beyond it the barton and what was until 1875 the Old Parsonage. In 1820 the rights of the Manor passed from the Bishops of Winchester to Thomas Southwood of Lowton House, Lord of the Manor.

Arthur Edgell Eastwood J.P. lived at Leigh Court from 1902. He was one of two chief landowners here at that time, the other being Ernest Arthur Mattock of Lowton House. Leigh Court was similar to Leigh Farmhouse. It was also the Manor House until it burnt down in 1837. The present Leigh Court was then built on the site.

The village here this side of the church is called Angersleigh, and the crossroads below the church is called Lowton.

The children of the parish attended school at Lowton by 1889.

St Michael's and All Angels' Church: the day I visited this little

church the sun was brilliant in a clear blue sky and there was a feeling of absolute peace. It nestles at the foot of the hills and the words that came to me were, "I will lift up mine eyes unto the hills, from whence cometh my strength". I once asked a man what his religion was, he said "I believe in the mountains". I know what he meant.

The Manor was given by the West Saxon Kings to the Bishops of Winchester. The church dates from the early 12th century. In the year 1120, when the Priory was formed in Taunton, William Giffard, Bishop of Winchester, confirmed the church of Leigh to his new foundation. The Priory then provided the priests for Leigh Church until 1300 AD. The people living in the Manor at that time were called "De Legh". The family who succeeded them was called "Aungier", hence Angersleigh. "Leigh" is also derived from "Leah" a pasture or clearing. The church is sixty-five feet long and seventeen feet wide. It has changed slightly over the years; restoration has been done especially in the 19th century by the Reverends Tucker and Baillie. An arch was built over the chancel, the floor was raised, the porch was turned into a vestry and new windows were put in. The present altar is a wooden one dating from 1886. There was a stone altar previously, but it has disappeared. The pews in this little church are the most highly polished I have seen in any church and I could understand the love that the cleaning ladies had put into it. The font appeared to be the oldest relic. By 1931 there were five bells in the church. There is one called the "Jesus Bell" which was cast in Exeter in 1430 AD. It had a Latin inscription; "Est michi collatum I.H.S. istud nomen amatum", – translated "That beloved name of Jesus, is bestowed on me". There are sixteen Jesus bells in Somerset. The Blackdowns claim four of them – the others are at Staple Fitzpaine, Otterford and Thurlbear. There is a plaque on the wall commemorating Arthur Edgell Eastwood of Leigh Court, for 49 years' faithful service producing much of the wood carving. There are two beautiful Apostle windows each depicting six Apostles. The first one has Thomas, Matthew, James minor, Jude, Simon and Mathias. The second window has St Peter, Andrew, James, John, Phillip and Bartholomew. The words underneath them read: "Go ye therefore and teach all nations".

The organ is very small and was given by Mr and Mrs Eastwood in 1904. It was restored by George Osmond of Taunton. Entering the church there is a small door on the right leading to the Belfry, the step is worn down with so many feet over the centuries. In 1921 an illuminated book was given by public subscription, containing the names of the parishioners who served in the Great War, 1914-18.

Another touch which I found here and no-where else: a little red light is always burning in the Sanctuary, this is a reminder that God is present.

Lowton:
Lowton Manor House, which was previously Lowton Farm House, was mainly built in the reign of Queen Anne, and was the home of the Southwoods and the Mattocks, Lords of the Manor of Taunton Deane.

In front of the house was the old Mill, there is still a mill wheel from medieval times. This is noted as one of the wonders of the Hills. Lowton and its crossroads lie at the bottom of Leigh Hill and were once very busy with the forge, village shop, Post Office and Dame's school.

Not far from this house is Howleigh. Here there is an ancient Field Strip, seen one day from an aerial photograph.

Paradise:
half way up Leigh Hill after passing the two tracks on the left which lead to the reservoirs of Leigh and Luxhay there is a turning on the right. Near here was a cluster of houses which was known as Paradise. These were demolished sometime around World War I to make way for another reservoir. The remains of the cottages can still be seen as the reservoir was never built and now after two exceptionally hot dry summers it has been suggested that the plans should be looked at again.

Chelmsine:
a handful of houses and a small chapel which looked redundant. One lady told me that she had a friend who visited her, and this friend was a medium. When standing at the crossroad she shivered and felt a force which told her there had been many deaths there. On relating this story later she was told it had once been the site of another gallows.

Quants Reserve:
on the right hand side when climbing Leigh Hill, and lying at the bottom of Buckland Wood, is Quants Reserve. This is a reserve of 34 acres purchased by the Somerset Trust for Nature Conservation in 1986. There are many species of flora, but the birds are the great interest here. Seen recently are the Garden Warbler, Blackcap and Nightingale. It is interlaced with footpaths and near the top are three tunnel entrances. Although now closed and owned by the Wessex Water Authority, they house a colony of bats.

The Merry Harriers:
this 15th century Free House at the top of Leigh Hill was first built in 1492 and it has exposed beams. It sits on the infamous Forches Corner where ambushes and hangings took place. The plot was once a gallows, as far as I could find out, last used during Monmouth's time. The road now running along the front of the Merry Harriers was first a footpath and then a drove road in ancient times, growing as the traffic grew. It has always been known as the High Ridge Road.

Forches Corner:
opposite the Merry Harriers and on top of Quants Reserve is a conservation area and picnic site, known as Buckland Wood. The wild flowers and plants are numerous. The walk through the wood, which also has a bridle path, lies on the west side of Leigh Hill itself. These are ancient woods and here will be found hanging oaks (a hanging wood is

57

woodland growing on a very steep hill) of which the acorns were used for feeding swine. The hedge which runs down the side of the road also forms the boundary between the parishes of West Buckland and Pitminster. There has probably been woodland here since the ice cap receded in 10,000 B.C. when forests began to form.

Kingsmead Caravan Site: Off the beaten track this is another beautiful spot for a quiet rest.

West Buckland: a stream from Luxhay Reservoir runs through this village. Here a hoard of jewels was discovered about a century ago, by workmen digging a drain.

The Manor of West Buckland was given to Athelm, Bishop of Wells in 909 AD, when the Bishopric was created. It remained in the possession of the Bishops until 1548. Then the lands were split; some went to the Crown and then to Sir James Fullerton. After the Battle of Waterloo, the Manor passed to the Duke of Wellington. The land has now been sold again in parts to several people.

King Ina fought a battle at West Buckland. At this time, in 710, Geraint was the Lord of Devon (see Simonsburrow). Ina's brother was killed and buried on Buckland Hill, but the barrow has long disappeared. An account of this battle says that the streams ran knee high in blood.

St Mary The Virgin: Here a cutting taken from the Holy Thorn at Glastonbury flourishes. (I am afraid I agree here with Daniel Defoe, who wrote: "Of the Holy Thorn, many absurd accounts have been given.")

There was an early Norman church on this site and the present Church was restored in 1891. It was built in the shape of a cross. The tower can be seen as a landmark for miles around. In the porch above the door is a niche which once held a statue, which was probably lost at the Reformation. Also in the porch is a medieval water stoup. The chancel is slightly askew to the right, to symbolise the fact that Christ died on the cross and his head fell to the right. The chancel arch is believed to date from 1250. The font is of indeterminate age, but is extremely old, probably Norman. It is made of Purbeck stone, although the base is more modern. By its side there is a beautiful Paschal Candle which is lit at each baptism. Also here on the walls will be seen again a Baptismal Roll, this one dates from 1964.

One lovely stained glass window in the north aisle is a memorial to the Thomas family and their sons; the dates are 1839-1881. This was put there in 1891 by Norris & Co. The remaining glass windows were made by John Toms of Wellington (see St John the Baptist, Wellington, earlier in this book). The window of the north chapel is square and does not match any others; it dates from about 1450. This north Chapel used to be the chapel for residents of Gerbestone Manor, but now it is locked and used as a vestry. The organ is situated also in the north aisle, blocking off the former north doorway; this was done because it made the church cold and draughty. The church register dates from 1538. There are two Queen Anne chairs in the sanctuary. There are Norman fragments embedded in the walls.

Gerbestone Manor: The north chapel in West Buckland Church was kept for the family residing at this house. The building is pre-Reformation with traces of a 13th century building in the south wing and was modernised in the time of Elizabeth I, and then again in 1925. In 1581 John Perry left to his wife Elizabeth "all such wenscott, bordes, bed steeds and hangings within my house at Gerbestone, together with all the farm stock and growing crops".

The Black Bird Inn: This 16th century hostelry was a coaching inn, on the Exeter to London run, a hundred years before even the Truman Brewery was set up in Spitalfields in 1666. It now stands on the A.38 halfway between Wellington and Taunton. Judge Jeffreys stayed here, but one of its favourite characters was Mr Twoose who would come and drink sixteen quarts of ale before breakfast. He always had two plates for his meal, one for the meat and the other for vegetables. It was said that he had the strength of an ox, and would walk from Ham, where he lived, to West Buckland carrying a hundred weight sack of corn on each shoulder.

Heatherington Grange: another eating house situated on the A.38. It is also at the point on the road that the ghost of a figure dressed in a grey coat sometimes appears. He has been seen at various times since the 1950s and was possibly the victim of a road accident.

Sheppy's Cider Farm, Three Bridges: this is one of Somerset's top cider makers. Cider has been made here for over 200 years. It is a very interesting place to visit as they have their own museum, which I might add is free, and fascinating to anyone interested in machinery. There is also a farm shop which sells all the firm's products.

For hundreds of years every farm hereabouts had its own cider press. I can remember myself as a child walking into a barn which held a wooden screw press and smelling the apples and the straw as they were squeezed to get out the last drop of juice. I remember seeing dead mice and rats which had fallen into the big wooden vats holding the cider, seeing the farmers fish them out and throw them into the corner. In those days big joints of meat used to be thrown in to add flavour. Today of course the cider in places like Sheppy's is made under very clinical and hygienic conditions, but I wonder if it tastes quite the same to the perspiring farmer after a day in the fields.

Somerset produced more cider than any other county, but in the past there was much more production than there is today, in fact years ago cider was paid to farm labourers as part of their wages.

Castleman's Hill: Slightly east of Sheppy's is Castleman's Hill Farm (see Trull). The house is built of Triassic stone from Rumwell and Blue Lias. It was said that the Duke of Monmouth hid and slept here. If he did it must have been before the battle as history would suggest that he never came back this way after the rebellion.

Hamwood: from Trull, taking the road marked Dipford and then at the triangle the Cutsey road, you will soon come to Hamwood and its cheese shop. I found this unexpectedly on a hot sunny afternoon. I ventured in and found the owners very warm and welcoming. The house is very old, parts of it possibly 15th century. There is a coat of arms over the front door but whether they belong to Henry Smyth holder of Hamwood is not established. John Smyth of Hamwood had two seats in Trull Church in 1635. Hamwood passed to the Baker family in the 17th century. John Baker was registered as a "gent", and at the time of the Hearth Tax he owned thirteen hearths. Some of these were in cottages that belonged to him. John Baker died in December 1677 and there is a memorial in Trull Church to him and his baby daughter, which I have recorded under All Saints Trull. John Baker's son, also called John was fined six shillings, for swearing six times. The present owner Mr Grant is now making cheese and in the lovely cool cheese shop at the rear of the house I bought some of the best cheese my husband has tasted in a long time.

Cutsey House: this lovely old house is now a guest house with the traditional home farm attached. Guests are allowed free use of the library, billiard room, sitting room and more besides, whilst also having luxurious sleeping accommodation. Rough or clay pigeon shooting is available and (I smiled at this) you can go horse riding providing you bring your own horse.

Zaney: two of the cottages which belonged to John Baker were on a site attached to Hamwood, called Zaney or Serneys, again spellings of this varied. By 1842 they formed part of Hamwood Farm. In 1915 the cottages were made ready and received refugees from Belgium. The cottages were demolished in 1939 luckily, because a year later the Germans dropped a bomb on the site.

Chilliswood Farm: A plaque here bears the date 1594 and it is still

60

Hamwood, with coat of arms over front door and, below, *bench end, Trull, showing the stem and leaf edging.*

61

The pulpit, Trull.

mostly of the late 16th century despite being restored considerably in 1830. It has an excellent original roof.

Higher Dipford Farm: this six-hundred-year-old farmhouse has exposed elm beams and ingle-nook fireplaces. It is a working dairy farm and also an attractive guest house.

Trull: in the year 1308 the parish of Trull was known as Trendle, which means circle or ring. That year the Bishop of Bath and Wells, Walter Haselshaw, in his ordination of St. Mary Magdalen in Taunton, defined the duties of the vicar, which included having a resident priest for Trendle.

In the village in 1558 lived one George Bond, he amassed a great fortune through his talents and his industry. He became Lord Mayor of London and was eventually knighted. He was a great benefactor. His daughter Dyonisia married Sir Henry Winston of Standish, Gloucester, and they had one daughter Sarah who was their heir. She married John Churchill of Mintern, Dorset, their marriage produced a son, Winston Churchill and their grandson was John Churchill, the First Duke of Marlborough. In George Bond's will he stated that he had been born at Buckland.

The Duke of Monmouth crossed The Blackdown Hills, or rather came around the Hills, via Chard, Ilminster and Hatch, on his way from Lyme Regis to Taunton.

In 1785 AD there was a regular parish doctor who received the wage of four guineas per annum. One of the biggest scourges at that time was smallpox. New poor houses were built in 1802, these adjoined the churchyard.

In 1843 a Wesleyan College was built in this parish. In 1888 it was renamed Queen's College in honour of Queen Victoria. This is a private College and is controlled by a body of directors.

A small elementary school for children was erected in 1875 for Trull and Pitminster. An elderly lady told me that her mother went to this school in its early days and she had to pay one penny a week which was a lot of money then.

The old coach house has now been made into private residences and the public house is called the Winchester Arms, after the Bishops who held the Manor of Taunton.

Dipford is attached to Trull and as it suggests it was once a ford, water still rises high in the road after a storm causing havoc for motorists.

Kings Gatchell House: in the 17th century King James I stayed here and later, probably in the 1800s the house was renamed Kings Gatchell. This 'T' shaped building built sometime in the 16th century was previously called Southwick House. In the main bedroom embossed in plaster is the

King's Coat of Arms. In its time it was a coaching inn, and part of the cobbled coach yard is still in existence. This is now a private residence. Across the road a younger house is called Gatchells and that accommodates a Country Club.

Behind Kings Gatchell is another very old cottage called Vine Cottage.

All Saints' Church: this is a beautiful and interesting church to visit.

Until the year 1836 the outside walls of the church were stuccoed and limewashed. The medieval builders used mostly grey Triassic sandstone, quarried at nearby Rumwell.

The pulpit is a great treasure and now said to be of national importance; it is half a pentagon and it dates from the 16th century. It is thought that the carved figures on the pulpit were hidden under the floor at the time of the Puritans. The smaller figures and the woodwork were not thought valuable enough to hide and therefore they did not escape destruction. The Saints on the pulpit are St. John the Evangelist, Pope Gregory, St. Augustine of Hippo, St. Jerome and St. Ambrose.

The best stained window here is called the Dragon Window. It is a small square window and can be found in the south wall of the sanctuary. The window was made in the late 15th century but it has been extensively restored and a careful look will reveal that the figure of St. Margaret is more modern. This window is so called because a dragon was said to live in the region of Castleman's Hill, terrorising the district, and making human kind its diet. It was eventually slain by a valiant knight. There is a dip in the field where the fight supposedly took place. In the window will be seen St. Michael, St Margaret and St George all slaying the beast.

Opposite the Dragon Window is another matching square window which would have been on the outside of the church until the Victorians built a vestry on that corner in one of their restorations.

The east window shows the crucifixion and if you look closely at Mary in the side light you will see that she has tears in her eyes.

In 1476 the churchyard cemetery was consecrated; before this people were buried at the Priory.

In the 16th century even the poorest people felt it their duty to leave some money to the church. So it was in 1535 that Anthony Phillips left his best coat to the church, he also left 2d to Wells Cathedral. On his death his whole estate was only worth 13s 8d.

In 1573 the chalice was melted down and made into a communion cup. The cup took less silver, but unfortunately it is no longer in the church. The oldest piece remaining is a flagon dated 1731.

In the 16th century there were three appointed Church Wardens, who would hold office for a year, when three more would be elected. The post of church warden was not an enviable one, carrying responsibilities for the maintenance of the church and the raising of sufficient money to support the poor. Most of this money came from the parishioners, who had to pay a church tax, collected by the wardens. Working alongside these officials were a sexton and a clerk, which most churches also had. The sexton dug the graves and kept the churchyard tidy. The clerk had to keep order during the services and also sing a loud 'Amen', after each prayer and hymn. He was responsible too for entering all church ceremonies in the Register, which dates from 1670.

It is interesting to note that in 1635 women were labelled the wives of men, but they never sat with their husbands in church. This was the case in most churches about that time. Here the pews in the south aisle, or behind the "Crosse Alley", between the north and south doors, were given over to the women, Labourers, menservants and lowly males used to sit in the north aisle. The clergy and the gentry would sit at the front. When the service was over and the final hymn was being sung, the privileged would walk back down the aisle and the poor congregation would bow and curtsey to them.

There is an interesting epitaph here to a member of the Baker family of Hamwood, which I think is well worth recording. The baby was born on November 6th 1658 and was buried on December 29th 1658.

> A spotless child lies here within,
> Whome fate allowed not time to sinne,
> But after death had giv'n its rest,
> Christ tooke into his arms and blest,
> Where now amongst that quire on high,
> It sings its owne sweet lullabie,
> The mother to its earthie bed,
> Bequeathed this stonie coverlet.

Between the 15th and 16th centuries, one of the most famous wood carvers in Somerset was Simon Warman. His initials appear on several pieces of carving around the Taunton area. In Trull Church most of these beautifully carved pews are his work and his initials appear at the end of the north aisle. This is something else of interest to look for when visiting Somerset churches. Simon particularly liked foliage and birds. One of his bench ends in this church displays a large "W" held up by two birds. Not all the bench ends in Trull are by Simon Warman, but you can distinguish his by his trade mark, which is the edging. He always carves a stem, crossed at intervals by a leaf.

Simon also liked carving the Green Man. This is the head of a man with foliage coming out of his mouth and ears. He denotes fertility, and you will find him somewhere in most churches; sometimes he appears in stone, worked by the stonemasons. Other bench ends in this church were carved by John Waye Clarke, another famous woodcarver.

Some church restoration took place in 1862–3 by the Rev. W. Jeffrey Allen M.A. of Gatchell House at the cost of £250 taken from a charity fund left by some unknown person in the reign of James I. (Could it have been donated by James I himself, when he stayed at Gatchells. See Kings Gatchell.) The chancel was restored at the same time by F.W. Newton. In 1890 further restoration took place.

Look for a gravestone in the churchyard to Oliver Cromwell – not *the* Oliver Cromwell, but his namesake.

The author Mrs Ewing, who wrote *Jackanapes* among other stories, is here. Some of the bells were made in clay moulds in the churchyard. They have a perfect tone. Also in the churchyard are some well preserved stocks. They were mainly used in the 17th century when it was the job of the constables to round up any thieves or minor criminals and put them in the stocks where they were pelted with rotten eggs and fruit. Constables then were high ranking officials of a royal household or manor house, who were employed to keep the peace. The cross was erected by public subscription to the 17 men who lost their lives in the Great War.

Footpath T.D.B.C.: this is a circular footpath of about two miles, so if you have a car it is a good idea to leave it at Trull and start from there. Enter by the park gates. Note the Lion and the Unicorn on the posts which date from George V. Enter the playing field and follow the worn path with the hedge on your right hand side. Follow this around the top of the field, and notice that the footpath leaves the field behind the football changing rooms, diagonally from where one entered. This footpath in a straight line between the houses and gardens, comes out in Amberd Lane, Staplehay. Turning left and walking down Amberd Lane until coming to a small bridge, the footpath enters into a field on the left. Keeping the hedge on the right, one soon comes to a stile which crosses over a waterfall, known locally as Victoria Falls. It is best to do this walk after heavy rain, when the water is gushing downstream or in the winter when the water is frozen into icicles, then the full effect of the water can be seen. Continuing across the top of the falls and into the next field, the path is well defined and eventually leads into a wood and across the stream again. This rises back into the playing field where the walk started. For a longer walk, when in Amberd Lane, instead of taking the footpath on the left by the bridge, take the footpath on the right before the bridge, into the fields once more. This goes across the motorway bridge, past Poundisford Park and across two more fields to Pitminster, where a deserved drink in the Queens Arms can be enjoyed.

Staplehay: a hamlet, being adjacent to Trull, it is the home of Trull

*Queen's College, Trull and the police head-
quarters at Canonsgrove.*

Tennis Club. The only public house here is The Crown.

Canonsgrove: this large house is now a training centre for the Police. Sir Robert Peel formed the Police Force in 1829. As I walked along the road two grey squirrels were playing in one of the large trees in the grounds. They can be destructive creatures stripping bark from the trees, not to eat, but to suck out the sap, but they are very intelligent and lovable and will become quite friendly with humans. They also make their nests out of the stripped bark and the female has a forty-day pregnancy.

The house was built in 1825 and is of Regency design. Originally it included stables, a coach house and a walled kitchen garden but these have been demolished to make way for Police training buildings. The house was a private residence but it was taken over by the Air Ministry during World War II and used to accommodate fighter pilots who were carrying out operational flights from nearby Culmhead, mainly from Polish, Australian and Czechoslovakian Air Forces.

After the war the house was refitted as a school. It was a Boys' approved school for a short period but was taken over again as a private residence in 1946.

The Somerset Constabulary took over the house in June 1963. There were several pets' gravestones found during redevelopment and two of them have been left on view. One is dated 1871 and the other 1923.

The ghost of Canonsgrove is an old lady called Miss Reynolds who was murdered and hidden under the floor boards of what is now the general office.

Amberd Farmhouse: this former farmhouse is now a private residence and is dated about 15th century. The walls are mainly cob on a stone base with an internal batter. The roof is still thatched. Although this house has been substantially modernised two of the old windows remain. Smoke blackening indicates that this old long house was once single storeyed. Lower parts of the roof trusses are obscured but it is possible that they are jointed crux.

Amberd House: Adam de Amingford has been traced back to 1232 in the Pipe Rolls, and he is probably the man that gave this area its name. The site of this house has been inhabited since 1457, when Robert Bale sold half a virgate of bondland and four acres of overland to Richard Colbrond. The house in its present form dates from 1804. At one time this was the home of the Treats or Trotts. Three bells in Pitminster Church, dated 1630 were cast at the order of the vicar, Walter Travers. The question of payment for these bells caused much discontent amongst the parishioners. Richard Treat or Trott, who led the discontent, was baptised in Pitminster Church

in 1584. He emigrated to Connecticut in 1637 with his wife Alice and nine children, and there became a leader of the English Colony. His son became Governor of the Colony of Connecticut. One of his numerous descendants signed the Declaration of Independence. The story can be read on a brass plaque on the north wall in Pitminster Church. Doctor Francis Woodforde obtained the property sometime after 1861 and by 1865 had converted it into a female mental asylum. It remained so until 1879. In 1883 it was owned by Vice Admiral V Grant Hickley J.P. In 1951 Amberd House was bought by Clarence Harris who divided it into three separate dwellings.

Brown Elm: sited on an unclassified road above Trull is Brown Elm, just a few houses, with a triangle in the road, not with an elm tree on it but a horse chestnut. This fork leads either back into Staplehay or on towards Poundisford House. Following the latter road Taundean Kennels will soon be found, just for aristocats and well-bred dogs. This is where the M.5 Motorway cuts through the hills.

Poundisford Park: a pound is an enclosure and in 1210 the Bishop of Winchester maintained a park of about one hundred acres at Poundisford. A herd of deer was kept here especially for his sport inside this enclosed park belonging to Taunton Castle. The fence around such a park was called the park pale. King John visited Taunton about this time and it is thought that the Bishop of Winchester invited him to hunt at Poundisford. In the year 1211, King John sent deer from Hereford to restock the Park. Another ancient wonder of the hills is here, as part of the enclosing fence still remains.

In the early 16th century the Park, which then only had a lodge for the keeper, passed from the Bishop of Winchester to John Soper who surrendered part of the lease to Roger Hill. William Hill his eldest son was away working as a merchant at the time, and Roger's second son set about building a house by the lodge, now called Poundisford Lodge. When William returned home he found that his father had died and his younger brother was firmly in situ. He went to John Soper and induced him to part with a lease for a piece of ground in 1546, and then he set about building "as good a house or better as quickly". Poundisford Park is about half a mile further down the road from the Lodge, and this explains why there are two large similar houses. This Tudor house, built in the shape of an "H", because Henry VIII was on the throne at the time, has three storeys. The Hills remained in ownership until Dr. Simon Welman MD bought the house in 1706. His brother, Isaac Welman, became High Sheriff of Somerset in 1710. The Welmans remained here until the Helyars, who occupied the Lodge, bought the house in 1869. They didn't actually live in the house but let it to various tenants and this was the time when the house became most neglected. A.W.Vivian Neal MC DL JP who became High Sheriff of Somerset in 1943, bought the house in 1928 and lovingly brought it back to its original glory. The Vivian Neals still live in the house and open it to the public. The owners themselves show people around and point out in loving detail different aspects which would probably otherwise be missed.

It is set on the unclassified road between Trull and Pitminster. Walking along from Trull (note the Victorian letter box in a wall) one comes to an entrance with pillars topped with lions. This was the original entrance to the house, but one of the owners decided to turn it back to front and put a front entrance at what was then the rear, from which the view of The Blackdowns is more pleasant. They did away with the original drive and built a ha ha. Further down the road, still on the right, there is a drive marked 'Poundisford House' and 'Well House Restaurant', which is now the entrance. Turning the house around in this way explains why the lovely old lead water butt dated 1671 is in the front. Also in the garden is a 17th century gazebo. Most of this house dates back to Henry VIII; it is well preserved and has had very little alteration, although some additions were made in both the 17th and 18th centuries.

It has moulded plaster ceilings and it exhibits some fine china, furniture and costumes. The moulded ceiling in the hall has got the initials of William Hill and his wife etched among the stars and pendants.

In 1570, the Minstrel's Gallery was enclosed because of the cold. Of extra interest is the muniment room, where in the Middle Ages parchments, documents and papers were always kept and used. In houses such as this, such a room will be found adjacent to the large fireplace or chimney. This kept all the papers dry and saved them from rotting. These big old houses took a lot of heating and with so many forests all around them, big log fires were kept going nearly all the year round. This is a house well worth visiting.

The most famous person to have stayed here was Queen Anne, wife of James I. All her ladies in waiting stayed with her, and consequently there was no room for James and his gentlemen, so they all stayed at Southwick House, Trull, which afterwards became known as Kings Gatchell. In 1645 Goring's troops broke in and ransacked the muniment room. Roger Hill, the owner, was away at the time, but he was an ardent Parliamentarian. He became M.P. for Bridport that same year and sat in the Long Parliament. The Hills were not at Poundisford very often, preferring to spend most of their time in London.

On the stairs there is a portrait of George Vivian in the costume he wore to Albania. He also travelled extensively to Greece, Italy, Spain and Portugal.

The old kitchens which were a separate building, are now a restaurant called the Well House.

Pitminster:
Anciently known as Pipeminstre, Pitminster is a parish in the hundred of Taunton, given by King Hardicnute to the Church of Winchester. It comprises the following hamlets of Blagdon, Leigh, Fulford, Trendle, and Duddlestone.

In 1351 a terrible darkness came to Pitminster. This was the Black Death. It swept through the area unmercifully and no village was left untouched.

At the dissolution of the monasteries the Manor of Blagdon, the grange of Barton, the refectory and advowson of Pitminster, Corfe and Trull, the Manor of Middlecot and various other parcels of land, all belonging to Taunton Priory were granted to Humphrey Colles by King Henry VIII. After Monmouth's defeat a double locked wooden coffer was found, full of French coins, in a nearby farmhouse.

At one time in 1818 Pitminster had four reading schools and one writing school in various houses, for about seventy children. By 1861 there was a National School for boys and girls, where a Sunday School was also held. There were two maltings and a tannery.

Electricity first came to Pitminster in 1932 although electric lighting had been demonstrated in the church in 1898 driven by the Barton Grange dynamo.

The Public House is the Queen's Arms, this building is of many ages, but the oldest existing part is the mill which is actually mentioned in the Domesday Book. Another place worth stopping at for refreshment before walking on. I suddenly realise why I didn't lose any weight on this walk.

St Mary's and St Andrew's Church:
a thousand years ago Pitminster was the centre of a vast estate and this was its Minster Church. In 854 AD, these lands were given to Taunton to come under the Taunton Minster. A 'minster' church would have a college of priests who would cover surrounding churches and chapels. In about 900 AD the Manor of Taunton Deane was passed to Bishop Denewulf, Bishop of Winchester. The church here was given to Taunton Augustinian Priory in 1158 AD, along with its chapels at Corfe and Otterford. The first recorded vicar was William in 1297.

The present church was built of local grey stone during the 13th century, on the site of an old Saxon church. The tower and part of the nave is over 700 years old. This is another unusual tower, worth a look, with a normal square base, an octagonal belfry and a lead covered spire which is said to lean.

The Register dates from 1544.

At St. Mary's and St. Andrew's Church, John Colles, the grandson's tomb: four daughters, twin babies, one at head and below *Birchwood Chapel, still in use and lit by candles.*

There is a big tomb effigy here to Humphrey Colles; he was High Sheriff of Somerset in 1557 and died in 1570. His effigy has been moved to the back of the church, but it was formerly over his grave in the chancel.

His son John's tomb is in the chancel and there are six children kneeling in front of it. One of them, his eldest son John, has his own tomb opposite; the eldest daughter has a skull in her hands. Here is a connection with another great estate, as John's wife Anne came from Longleat. She was a daughter of Sir John Thynne.

Across the chancel on John's tomb, four daughters are kneeling in front of his monument. Here also is his wife Elizabeth and there are twin babies lying one at Elizabeth's feet and the other at her head. The girls have no skulls, so they outlived their parents. The babies were twin boys, one was stillborn and the other died while still a baby. Elizabeth was daughter and heir to Humphrey Wyndham.

It is very interesting to see what can be made of the inscriptions on them all.

John Colles, the second, the grandson, died on September 3rd 1627, he was only 45 years old. His wife Elizabeth died aged 48 in 1634. Of his daughters, Elizabeth, Anne, Margaret and Dorothy, three of them married into well-known families. Anne married William Portman, Margaret married Sir Gerard Napier, and Elizabeth married John Coventry. John was the eldest son of Lord Thomas Coventry, Lord Keeper of the Great Seal of England in the reign of Charles I.

There are three aisles and the pews are carved only down the middle aisle. The 15th century font is of Bere stone and is about the oldest relic left. There is a spiral staircase to the rood loft which dates from 1400.

Sir Gilbert Scott, one of the most famous architects of the period, restored this Church, he moved the south porch and rebuilt the north aisle. He left a stone pulpit, but this was moved to Hemyock Church in 1952. The present Jacobean carved pulpit is one of a very few with a canopy, it is well worth a good look.

Here there are windows with fragments of medieval glass left in (see stained glass earlier in this book); they are to be seen in the Lady Chapel.

It is interesting to see that the organ blower was worked by water power from the stream, until electricity took over.

I did particularly like the north west window, which is dedicated to Hilary Nora Hobhouse, who died on active service in 1946 aged 21 years. It depicts all the things she enjoyed in her life: horse riding, ski-ing, and lots of animals.

There is a ring of eight bells dating from 1630 right up to 1978, when the final two were added. A new steel bell cage was also erected in place of the wooden one.

On the staves are old brasses which depict the Lamb and Flag, symbol of the risen Christ and adopted by the Friendly Society (Quakers). These belonged to the former Parish Friendly Society formed to help the poor and sick. There were of course no social services.

In the north transept is a second piscina. There is a memorial on the wall in memory of Arthur Vivian Neal MC DL who died on 1st February 1962. He was High Sheriff of Somerset in 1943. The Vivian Neals now live in Poundisford Park.

By the door there is also a brass of Richard Treat (alias Trott) and his descendents (see Amberd House).

In 1953, Major Barrett, churchwarden for many years offered to give a new east window. Unfortunately he was killed in a tragic accident and the window was forgotten. The old window was in a very poor condition by 1984 and so the Church invited Jane Grey to design a new window. There was generous help from America and the window, named the "Calling of Andrew", was installed in 1989. It depicts Jesus calling Andrew saying "Follow me, I will make you fishers of men".

It is well designed and adds great beauty to the church. As in all these churches each generation leaves its mark.

Outside in the churchyard are the stone crosses, the angels, the flat stones and the vaults. The author Alexander Kinglake died in 1891 and is buried in the churchyard.

Funeral hatchments, diamond-shaped wooden painted boards, hold the coat of arms (armorial bearings) of the deceased. They were introduced for noted persons in the 17th century. They were hung on the dwelling house at the time of death before being removed to the church.

Corfe: wherever one is in Taunton, or driving along the B.3170, South Road towards Corfe, one becomes aware of four trees dominating the skyline on The Blackdown Hills. Once there were five trees but now there are only four and they have been christened Matthew, Mark, Luke and John after the four Apostles by the forestry men. The last time I spoke to a member of the Forestry Commission they were having trouble with Mark, as it was not flourishing like the others. I believe it has had the equivalent of a dose of "Baby Bio" since then. While on the subject of trees, two other old named trees were the two pollarded elms which once flanked the entrance to the church. They were called Gog and Magog by the inhabitants, but sadly they died and have since been felled. The Saxon word "Corf" means a cutting through the forest. The pipe rolls, started in 1208 AD, meant that from then on records of the area were well kept. Soon after this Corfe became part of the Hundred of Poundisford.

Electricity first came to Corfe Church in 1898 powered by the Newton dynamo from Barton Grange. The main part of the village received electricity in 1927.

The old mill at the rear of the church is now a small industry called Trout Press Ltd, design and print. The stream which runs through the village is called Broughton Brook.

Hayne was once a Royal Hunting Lodge, Brook Farm was a Saxon mill and Church Cottages were an old long house. Now, at nearly the end of the twentieth century, the Village school has disappeared, and the doctor and the Post Office have actually gone during the two years it has taken me to walk The Blackdowns and write this book. The Village hall also has just been knocked down, but another one is being built on the same site.

The cricket matches used to be played in a field opposite Flyboat Farm, which was part of Barton Grange. It was made by Francis Wheat Newton for the enjoyment of his own family as well as the villagers. After this a pitch was used at the rear of the Queen's Arms at Pitminster and then it moved again to Sellicks Green in Blagdon. Arthur Newton was a cricketer of some renown having kept wicket for Somerset for about thirty years and also playing for England. Flyboat Farm was so named because the place lies low and therefore very prone to flooding.

There were mines and quarries here for employment years ago producing zinc and calamine.

The White Hart: from Saxon times this was part of the Manor of Taunton which was held by the Bishops of Winchester until 1822 when it was sold. In 1566 the land was part of a farm held by John Gentle. In 1632 the piece of land on which the pub is built was conveyed by Edward Hodder to Elizabeth Colles of Barton Grange. On her death in 1634 it went to her daughter Elizabeth Dodington, widow, who then married John Coventry. His father was Keeper of the Great Seal of King James I. The property then fell on hard times during the Civil War when Blake held Taunton, George Jervis the owner then had to raise a Mortage of £42.8s.0d. on the property from Francis Kimberley. When he did not repay this debt, Kimberley seized the land and sold it to William Pullman of Taunton. By 1751 an inn was established on this land and it was first recorded as being called The White Hart Inn in 1859.

Barton Grange: this once beautiful house was situated between the villages of Pitminster and Corfe. The Prior held the large farm of 140 acres in 1158, the barns and buildings disappeared with the dissolution in 1539, but the fishponds remained. With Henry VIII now becoming the head of the Church of England, the Priory lands were all divided and sold off. A new Tudor mansion was built here in 1550 when a very wealthy lawyer of Gray's Inn, known as Humphrey Colles, was granted the estate. Humphrey became High Sheriff of Somerset in 1557; he died in 1570. His son and grandson, both called John, each became High Sheriff of Somerset in

their day (see Pitminster Church). In 1644-5 when the Royalist soldiers stayed in nearby Orchard House another garrison was installed here; by that time the house belonged to John Coventry, husband of Elizabeth Colles. He was a zealous Royalist. Not far away in Poundisford Park, Roger Hill was a supporter of Cromwell and he was to become Baron of the Exchequer in the coming Commonwealth. (Descendant of the Roger Hill mentioned earlier). In 1692 Smart Goodenough bought the estate from the Coventry family; he became High Sheriff of the County in 1692 and died in 1721, the estate then passed to his nephew Francis Milner Newton, who was first Secretary of the Royal Academy; among the many guests he entertained was Gainsborough. The estate had increased to 2,214 acres by 1895. The Church renovation and the elementary school were both accredited to the wealth of the Newton family. F.W. Newton also presented about an acre of ground near the church for use as a recreation field, to commemorate Queen Victoria's Golden Jubilee on 20th June 1887, and is called "The Queen's Acre".

The major part of the house was demolished in 1931, leaving only the old Tudor wing still standing. The servants' quarters and the stable block have now been converted into pleasant residences.

St Nicholas's Church, Corfe: The first reference to Corfe Church was in 1158 when Henry of Blois, then Bishop of Winchester, gave the church at Pitminster, and its chapels at Corfe and Poundisford, to the Priory of St Augustine. We know that there was a place of worship on this site during Norman times. The stone building's transitional Norman style was completely restored in 1842 by Mr E Ferrey, Diocesan architect. Further work was done in 1858, when the tower was moved and the aisles were lengthened by C.E. Giles. The font is Norman with Saxon features, as are the corbels and a portion of the chancel walls.

On the south wall is a big wooden coat of arms, this example is of the House of Hanover and is dated about 1801. When Henry VIII made himself head of the Church of England, he liked to see his coat of arms exhibited in all his churches. When Charles II came to the throne he made it compulsory. The practice gradually disappeared by the time of George III's reign. Corfe parishioners are happy to have this one as there are only a hundred or so left now in the County of Somerset. Earlier this century a chandelier was found hidden under a grating in the floor. No one knows why it was hidden, or how long it had been there; speculation has it that it was hidden from the Puritans. If so, why wasn't it found when the Church was restored? It is blue in colour and now it has been fully restored, it is a dominant feature of the chancel.

The church has a nave of four bays and two distinguished looking old faces look down from the corbels in the nave. The tower is at the north-west angle of the Church and in 1960 another bell was added, now making six altogether. In 1969 the floor of the chancel and sanctuary was relaid as a memorial to the husband of Mrs Barrington Moore. The raised floor also heightened the altar, which unfortunately now hides the wording in the memorial window behind the altar.

There is a beautiful rose window which was erected as a memorial in 1859 by five surviving Leigh children to their parents. Three of these children, Henriette, Barbara and Susan, were teachers and in 1906 the choir stalls were carved with their initials as a memorial to them and was paid for by their pupils. The organ was rebuilt in 1906.

This lovely homely little church is small enough to be filled absolutely with flowers on wedding days and festive occasions. The prime colours of blue and red in the windows and the blue chandelier are so bright and cheerful, and low down there is another array of bright colours in the many kneelers made by the people of the village.

One of the previous vicars here left his mark by forming the local cricket club.

Another thought here, whilst visiting these churches, is how much people were shorter in days gone by; a thought prompted by the doors to the towers and belfries in some buildings being so low, like this one at Corfe. Note how small some of the suits of armour are, although one of the reasons for this is that males were forced into military service at a much younger age, sometimes as young as twelve years old. In Durham Castle (no, that's not on The Blackdowns!) there is a whole row of suits of armour worn by a group of Cromwellian soldiers and the largest chest size is 38 inches. Another factor is that food was not so nutritious or plentiful in bygone years and consequently people did not grow to great stature.

A ham-stone cross was erected by the church as a memorial to the fallen in World War I.

Pickeridge: here is the famous golf course, lying five miles south of Taunton on the B.3170 Par 69/SSS 68/PRO. It is situated on Pickeridge Hill, a spur of The Blackdowns. It has 18 holes on downland, 5,927 yards long. The groundsmen do a wonderful job and are very meticulous. This was once a thriving mining area and quarry; it mainly mined calamine (zinc ore). It was the brainchild of the vicar of St Nicholas Church, Corfe, who enlisted the help of Frank Newton of Barton Grange, Arthur Newton, his brother, Captain Charles Fox and Mrs Lindley, his daughter, in 1892. It started as a private venture. They hired Mr Henry Fowler, who by 1896 had a well established course of nine holes, which now has increased to 18.

Fulwood: this small hamlet between Pitminster and Blagdon Hill was probably first occupied in the Bronze Age.

The Welmans from Poundisford Park became devout Evangelicals; they were Calvinistic Methodists and they built a chapel. The Congregational Chapel was erected here in 1732 and seats 180. This large square building is now empty and used as a furniture store.

The Wessex Water Authority have a pumping station here, to pump water from The Blackdown reservoirs.

Blagdon Hill:
Blagdon got its name from a Saxon word meaning Wolf Hill. Saxon Charter fixes the boundary of this Parish in the year 843 AD. It stretches around Blagdon Hill across to Lowton and back to Staplehay.

On Sellicks Green playing fields there is a stone which dates back to the Bronze Age. There is now a plaque on it which reads:

> Monolith, Erratic
> found 1972
> Near Bronze Age site at
> Fulwood, possibly
> a standing stone.

Its plaque was put there by Edward du Cann, M.P. for Taunton at the time. (Bronze Age – 2,400 BC-750 BC).

The Congregational chapel was erected in 1837 for Nonconformists and seats 100 people. The vicar used to come from Wellington but when the congregation dwindled it closed. It was used during the second world war as an overflow school for evacuees. It is now run by the Datchet Evangelical Fellowship.

The Friendly Society used to meet in a room in the Lamb and Flag, which is another good place to stop for refreshment. Opposite this establishment is the White Lion giving this small village the choice of two public houses.

The Mission Hall which nestles in the corner of a field next door to the Lamb and Flag was built in 1878 and seats 150 people. It was built as a small church for the Church of England as it was too far for some of the people of Blagdon to go to Pitminster. It too was used as an overflow schoolroom during the war. It closed some time ago and is used as a store room, now sadly the floor is rotting and it is falling into dilapidation.

The small triangular field by the Mission is the remains of the old village green. On the sloping hill is a wood of one hundred and twenty acres (see Priors Park).

Going up the hill, before reaching the 'S' bend, on the right there is Blagdon Hill Memorial, a large stone cross, 25 feet high, erected by parishioners for the nineteen men of the Parish who lost their lives in the Great War.

At the very top of the hill where the houses stand on the hillside and where Govier's lorries rest before each day's work at the quarries, one can find a small road going back sharply on the right. Here can be found a garden with a pump in it. This private residence was once one of Brierley's seven mission chapels on the hills.

Taunton Waterworks were founded in 1858; it was decided to bring the water from The Blackdown Hills. Blagdon reservoir was built in 1878, followed by Leigh Hill reservoir in 1893 and Luxhay reservoir in 1905.

Electricity first came to Blagdon in 1932.

Otterford Mills: the mills are in the widespread Parish of Otterford
down a lane on the left off the B.3170 just past School Farm. Only the house now stands but this fine building used to be a corn mill. The walls are very thick and built mainly of flint. A previous owner was said to live here and sleep on hay. It then became Crown property but now it has been sold privately.

I walked on down the narrow little lane towards Bishops Wood and in the hedge I found a family of wrens. I counted seven. It is lovely to find birds like these which have become so rare.

Birchwood: I deviated just a little at Otterford Mills to follow a signpost
marked Birchwood. This is in the widespread village of Otterford, but before the days of the motor car, because the parishioners here had so far to walk to church, either to St Leonards at Otterford or to St. Mary's at Buckland St. Mary, they decided to build a small chapel of their own. So in 1887 at the cost of £331 Clara Lance, sister of the Rector of Buckland St Mary, helped the people fund and build this church. I found this small charming little building quite by accident. It must surely be one of the smallest working Church of England establishments in the land. A lady kindly showed me where the key was and I went inside. There is no electricity and the services are all held by candlelight. The organist brings a small portable organ with him to each service. Services are still held here every three weeks. It is surrounded by a wall. A footpath winds its way behind this building and although it was only March a large pink rhododendron bush and a mass of spring flowers were in full bloom.

Bishops Wood: I walked through this charming village, with everything
so neat and tidy. The Candlelight Inn was built in the 17th century and was formerly called the New Inn. Bishops Wood is actually the village for Otterford, but Otterford itself is so widespread and scattered that the two appear unconnected. In 1791 John Collinson said about Otterford in

Antiquities of Somerset: "The houses are meanly built, and stand singly about the parish".

This village also has many alder trees, which, in years gone by, were used for clog making. The alder was also woven into sheets and used for the river beds.

In the field near here are remains of more lime kilns, which kept the local people employed for many years.

A chapel was erected here in 1874 for the Plymouth Brethren. Later purchased by George Brearly for the Blackdown Mission (see Brown Down). The old vicarage was designed by H.W. Brewster, a reputed Victorian Ecclesiastical Architect, for the Bishop of Bath and Wells in 1856. Bishopswood National School was erected in 1851 and a Sunday School was also held in it.

A Board School was built in 1882, not far along the road towards the Holman Clavel (mentioned earlier).

Chapter Three
The East End

Buckland St Mary: after walking past the Otterford Mill House and passing through Bishopswood, I came to this charming village and was surprised to find that it was Buckland St. Mary. The village is of Saxon origin and there was a church on the site of the present church in that period. "Bocland" was a Saxon word for land granted to nobles by Saxon kings. This may be where the name Buckland comes from, but another theory is that it derives from "Beoc" which is Saxon for beech; hence Beocan Londe or land of the beech tree. The Blackdowns are certainly well stocked with beech.

The early owners of the Manor were called Meriet. Katherine of Aragon passed by here after landing at Lyme Regis on her way to London to marry Prince Arthur. It would have been a very colourful and memorable day for the locals.

There was a mill here called Keats Mill which ground corn for over 200 years, but it is no longer working. From the 16th century a cattle and a toy fair were held here annually on the Wednesday and Thursday after the 20th September.

Opposite the Church is a well or drinking fountain, it is a small hamstone and flint shelter with a brick roof. There is now a tap to supply a drink. It is dated 1876 and was built at the expense of the vicar at the cost of £100. Inside is a plaque which unfortunately is unreadable. A new pet cemetery was opened in 1989 at Dingford Green Farm. Owners can have their pet buried in style complete with tombstone for a small fee.

The Lamb and Flag: this building was first licensed in 1837. Church meetings were held here in the 1840s and on May 5th 1844 the main topic was the taking down and rebuilding of the Church. The name "Lamb and Flag" also suggests that, like the Blagdon Hill pub of the same name, it was used by the Friendly Society.

Unfortunately January 1990 saw the closure of this establishment as a drinking house.

St Mary's Church: this church is well worth a visit as it is such a surprise both in its size and its profusion of figures of angels, saints and apostles. There have been three churches built on this site. The present one was built in 1863 by Benjamin Ferry and is made mainly of flint and ham stone. It was paid for by John Edwin Lance, who was rector between 1830 and 1885, in memory of his wife Louisa. He also built the school and the rectory. The similarity in the buildings is clear.

Edward II coins have been found in the foundations.

It has lych gates with the inscription "Open me the gates that I may go into them and give thanks unto the Lord". In the porch there is an old wooden board showing bequests left to the poor of the Parish since 1579. The last mention was in 1926. This was obviously kept from the previous church.

In the list of incumbents of the church, the first vicar mentioned was Richard Molyne in 1328. The vicar in 1371 was bailed for poaching. The records are well kept, except for a break of 50 years in the late 14th century, when the Black Death was rife in the country. One who must have been quite a character was Francis Hathway, who was brought to court and examined in 1664 by Henry Walrond Esq, Justice of Peace for Somerset, for allowing his spaniel bitch to draw out the throat of a man and kill him. The man was kept for a while in a pit and the dog was hung on an apple tree. In 1665 Francis was also reputed to be father of Francis, the base child of Mary Hopkins, and he was touched for the child's maintenance by the Justices.

In the 16th and 17th centuries a popular game was fives, played by bouncing a ball off a wall. Church towers were the obvious places to play and many vicars planted trees right by the tower to prevent the game being played. Here three youths were accused of trespassing and this caused a big fight, because whilst playing fives they trod on someone's cabbages. On the outside of the church are carvings in hamstone of a stag and a bull. There is also a lovely statue of Christ over the porch doorway and the crests of the Pophams and the Lances, both patrons of the living. The font and one of the windows were presents from the builder. There is a monument in the north wall to Lance's wife, who died young. This macabre memorial shows her rising from her coffin with her baby son – was she another victim of childbirth?

One of the windows was given by Lance's sister. The reredos also were erected in 1888 to Lance's memory; they are made of alabaster and marble and show seven angels carrying Christ at the Resurrection. Hamstone was used for the screens between the chancel and trancepts, with marble columns and white lias capitals. The chancel walls are made of Bath stone and Quantock stone. There is also a sedilla with three seats. The reredos, roof and the font all have rich carvings of saints, apostles and angels. The roof is oak and is made from trees actually grown on The Blackdown Hills.

There are twelve apostles in the clerestory carved out of Caen stone. The 20th century saw the former vestry turned into a chapel.

The tower was restored in 1969 and the organ was built by Sweetlands of Bath in 1972.

Between May and September 1978 the six bells were dismounted and sent to Whitechapel Bellfoundry for retuning. The cost of £4,350 was raised by the parishioners in less than a year. The stained glass windows are so numerous that it is difficult to pick out a favourite.

On a stone in the church there is this inscription:

> May all carters who read this,
> Take warning and never get in their wagons.

This was because one of the men who built the new church was riding on his wagon load of stone when the horses bolted; the wagon overturned and crushed the man to death.

The word "Lychgate" derives from the Anglo Saxon, "lych" meaning corpse or body. The beginning of the burial service started here from 1549, after the publication of the New Prayer Book.

In about the 16th and 17th centuries, when people were acquiring books and more people could read, it was a tradition on New Year's Day for all the family to sit around the table with the Bible. Each in turn would then open the book at random and point to a verse, which would then be looked at, discussed and turned into that person's horoscope for the coming year.

Beehive Farm: this farm, situated on the road to Neroche behind the village, has an interesting sculpture under the roof. It is a beehive, below which is the head of a man, and below that is a swirl of leaves with the date 1849 in the middle and the initials W.G. On asking the lady of the house what it all meant, she said at the time the church at Buckland St Mary was in the process of being built, the stone masons who carved all the figures stayed at this farm. The amount of carving work involved in the church meant it took years to build, and 1863 was when it was finished and consecrated. The head stone mason was William Grace and in their spare time they carved these creations and placed them in their present position. Parts of the house date back to the middle ages. The lady did not know why the farm was called Beehive, but when I learned the approximate age I thought that it was because many farms in the Middle Ages kept bees, as the honey was much in demand, as a sweetener and for mead, the wax for candles. The chimneys are very interesting and unique and well worth a look.

Dommett Wood – Moor: this is a small wood with some lovely deciduous trees and a Nature Reserve maintained by Somerset Trust for Nature Conservation. Local people find it very interesting to read

"Larksleeve", a best-seller by Patricia Wendorf, as it is based on the lives of the gypsies who used to frequent the wood, about a hundred years or more ago.

Dommett: this is a nice hamlet containing a couple of interesting farm houses.

The Eagle Tavern: the first reference to this public house seems to be in 1847, when six acres of land were purchased by Daniel Beale, who erected a dwelling house, which was to be used as an inn; locally it became known as the Eagle Tavern.

Staple Fitzpaine: the Fitzpaine family held the Manor until the Portman family were granted it by the Crown in 1600.

On 10th July 1643, Sir William Portman, the 5th Baronet, founded and built an almshouse or hospital for six poor people, one of whom was to be elected from Orchard Portman parish. The annual sum of £40 was paid out of the Orchard Portman estate to support this.

A school was opened in the village in 1823 for 14 pupils. The Portmans also opened a larger school in 1829.

The Manor House was built by Robert Lord Fitzpaine and it existed until the mid 16th century when it was destroyed by fire. It was beside the church, and later it was rebuilt and part of it became a poor house in the late 18th century.

Almost the whole parish was sold off by the Portmans in 1944 to pay death duties; they kept only forty acres of land and the Manor House. It is a rather impressive house, standing next to the Church, with its ham stone dressings, but most eye catching are the tall ham stone chimneys.

The local Public House is the Greyhound, dating back a few centuries, where a meal can be had.

While I write this book a row is going on over the erection of a mast, fifty metres high. It is proposed that the mast will stand on Mount Fancy Farm, the highest point on The Blackdowns. The application has been made by the Independent Broadcasting Authority.

There is another large stone here called the Devil Stone, again the well-worn story that the Devil was supposed to have stood on the hill and thrown it at the builders of the church accounts for it; this stone is also supposed to bleed if you prick it.

St Peter's Church: just walking up the path to this church there is quite much to note. First there is the obviously old yew tree. These trees are usually in the churchyard as it was communal ground. There were two essential reasons for planting yew. One was that the main weapon of

Beehive Farm: note the round chimneys and below, *Orchard Portman.*

Font, Buckland St. Mary: medieval cross, Thurlbear and, in the churchyard, Mary Chorley's six children.

defence at the time when most churches were first being built was the bow and arrow, and the best bows were made from yew. The other reason was that branches of yew were always carried by everyone on Palm Sunday as this was the tree that most resembled the Palm. The second thing to look out for going up this path is the old cross. Again there is no writing on it, but it looks very old and has one of the most elaborate tops of any of The Blackdown crosses. On the opposite side of the path are five very sad graves with crosses on the top. These belong to the Pollard family who nearly all died young.

When the master builder of the tower received two contracts to build two new towers, he faced a dilemma, and decided that he would let his top apprentice build the tower at Isle Abbots, while he himself built that of Staple Fitzpaine. When the jobs were finished the apprentice's tower at Isle Abbots was without a flaw. The master builder was a proud man, he had trained his boy well.

The perpendicular tower was built in 1470 with money given by the Duke of Northumberland whose family name was Percy. The tower has always been known as the Percy Tower.

The church is built of ham stone and blue lias. Below the parapets of the tower are four heraldic beasts, these pertained to the Percy family. There is a Norman doorway in the porch.

There are six bells in the tower, one of them is another Jesus bell. I found a plaque relating to one of the others, it goes as follows:

> This ring was augmented with a treble bell
>   from St. Mary's Church, Charlynch,
> In memory of Hugh Grabham – 1933-81.
> The bells, like angel voice speak peace to
>   every breast.

Originally this church was 12th century, but it was rebuilt in the mid 15th century. There was another restoration in the mid 19th century; the south aisle was added in 1841 and the vestry screen was brought from Bickenhall when that church was demolished in about 1847. The altar table was brought from All Saints Church, Curland, which is now being sold as a private residence.

The font cover in this church has a beautiful carving of the Pelican of Piety. The lightness of this church interior, I thought, is due to the lovely pine pews which are very unusual. In fact they are the first ones I have seen.

In January 1990 a hurricane, unusual in this country, badly damaged the Percy tower when ham stone pinnacles fell through the nave roof smashing a main arch beam and several medieval bosses.

A little girl was allowed to stay up late one night and also say grace when some family friends were coming to dinner. When eventually she stood up to say grace, she forgot her words.

"Do you remember what Daddy said at breakfast time when he said 'Oh God. . . .' '', her mother prompted.

The little girl's eyes lit up on remembrance. "Oh God why do we have to have those terrible people to dinner tonight," she prayed.

Orchard Portman: Orchard was the name of this family, which they
acquired from the fact that this area was covered in nothing but fruit trees.

Baldwin took the estate, and called himself Baldwin de Orchard. He passed the estate on to his son John in the reign of Henry III.

In Gerard's *Particular Description* of Somerset dated 1633, he wrote as follows:

> Which surely in my opinion well brookes the name, for it is sceated in a very fertile soyle for fruite, and the whole countrey thereabouts seems to be orchards, insomuch that all the hedgerowes and pasture groundes are full fraught with fruite to eat and make cider of.

It remained in the name of Orchard until the marriage of Christian Orchard of the female line, to a Walter Portman in the 15th century. This made these two merchant families among the richest in the country and the name Orchard Portman was adopted.

A William Portman was Sergeant at Law to Henry VIII and he died in 1555. At the time of the Monmouth Rebellion the Tudor Tavern belonged to Sir William Portman, another descendant, and it was here that Judge Jeffreys stayed.

In the General Election of 1688 Sir William Portman and John Sanford, for the Tories, set up their campaign in the Three Cups Hotel (now the County Hotel). They were determined to unseat the two Whig Candidates, so they employed an army of cudgel players from outside the town to come in and beat up any Whig voters they could find.

Taunton had two M.P.s until 1884 and the coming of the Redistribution Bill.

Orchard House was built in the 16th century and was demolished in 1843 because of an epidemic of typhus. The Portmans being one of the country's largest landowners had many residences. In the 1830s it was the Andrews family who lived in this house and when typhus broke out in 1837 they were the ones that fell victim.

Another Lord Portman served as Master of the Taunton Vale Foxhounds in 1927 and was largely responsible for the founding of Taunton Racecourse, he died in 1942 aged 44, and in 1944 most of the estate had to be sold off to pay death duties.

The royal sport of polo is played here. I walked into the club on a very hot Saturday afternoon. The entrance fee is £3 per car. No one noticed the lone hiker. There was a barbeque going on and it was a very friendly convivial atmosphere. There was a game in progress and I was surprised to find that there are only four players on each side and two referees. Not knowing anything about this game, I did learn quite a lot in the next five minutes from a very helpful young man. Although I would like to have stayed longer, it was soon onward again towards Wych Lake.

Now a new local Radio Station has opened here called Orchard.

St Michael's Church: this small church is perpendicular. The register of baptisms dates from 1538. It has a Norman north doorway and a late perpendicular west tower for which money was bequeathed in 1521 and 1532. An original south transept was replaced by a 11th century porch. Family pews were built in 1910. The Norman transept arch was then restored to its original position. The pulpit has Jacobean material. The chalice and cover are dated 1646 and the flagon and saucer are late 17th century.

There is a brass to Humphrey Colles dated 1693. The south aisle in which the brass was originally placed was removed in 1844.

In 1987 the parishioners of St Michael's held a meeting to plan the renovation of the Church. The families, made up from only six houses, spent one day a week repairing faults detected in the latest architect's report. These included a rotten floor, pews, and panelling, loose plaster and holes in the roof. Mr Roland Walker, Vice Chairman of the Committee, said that the cost of the work would run into several thousand pounds, so they decided to get on with it themselves and now meet every Tuesday.

Shoreditch: the forge still stands here and this is where the 18th June 1685 saw much activity as the Duke of Monmouth rode in to have his horses and cattle shod by William Upham the blacksmith.

Wych Lodge Lake: Sometimes called Witch Lake and sometimes Gingerbread. Loved by fishermen and hidden away in the woodland behind Orchard Portman, fishing in this pond is allowed and permits are available at £3 per rod per day. They can be purchased from Topp Tackle, Taunton, up to fourteen days in advance.

Stoke St Mary: this village, like others, completely surprised me with the charm and character of its old houses. One of the inhabitants was a William Bowyer who taught at Queen's University, Belfast. He retired to

Stoke St Mary and became well-known for writing poems about local events and places. He caught my eye as he had the same name as my father.

The Stoke chapel was erected in 1825. In 1990 the villagers celebrated the 165th anniversary. Noncomformist traditions in the village date back to 1669 when a survey taken revealed as many as one hundred worshippers. The movement declined during the 18th century and did not revive until about 1821. In 1853 the chapel was adopted as a preaching station for the newly formed Taunton Evangelist Society. In 1900 new glass doors were made and donated by Len Barry a local builder. They were dedicated by the pastor Mr K. Coles.

The public house is called the Half Moon. It is another of the places where I had several 'physical needs' breaks. This pub was burnt down in round about 1860, but was rebuilt as it is today. Up until the 1960s the landlord used to keep cows, turkeys and chickens to support the income.

St Mary's Church: this church was built in the 13th century, but a fire in the 19th century led to extensive restoration in 1864. At this time the south aisle and transept were also added. A square tudor window was at that time moved from the south wall and can now be found in the vestry. Also at the same time a window which was in the roof was lost. This was the light to a small gallery where the band played.

The squat tower is 13th century, as is the tower arch.

The outside of the church, except the tower, is lime-washed yellow; the stone is blue lias with ham stone dressings.

The font stem is 15th century and the bowl 19th century. The cover is carved with a lovely cross, in memory of William Burt of this parish, killed in France on 29th August 1918.

The doorway in the porch is also 15th century, with the moulding repeated from the stem of the font on the base of the door. The chapel was dedicated to St. Anne in 1972.

A 16th century bell cast by Roger Semson bears the letters A to N upside-down and backwards. It is one of only four such alphabet bells in the County.

West Hatch: the Manor was granted by King Richard I to the Church of Wells. The river Rag flows through this village, which is in the parish and hundred of North Curry. Also here is a branch of the R.S.P.C.A. and rather a famous one at that, for it is renowned for the removal of oil from stricken sea birds.

There were several quarries here which supplied blue lias stone, some of which was converted to lime. These kept people employed until well into the 20th century.

In the past, one of the chief crops grown here was the teasels, which supplied the wool industry. When this industry died out in the area the teasels were sent to the Yorkshire mills.

John Collinson in 1791 wrote the following:

> The following ancient custom is still observed here. The reeve or bailiff to the Manor, provides at the Lord's expense a feast on Christmas day, and distributes to each householder a loaf of bread, a pound and a half of beef and the like quantity of pork undressed, the same evening treats them to a supper.

A National School was built here in 1858 for 80 children.

The 16th century public house, The Farmers Arms, was once a cider house, and if one happens to be a guest at Three Elms Farm good meals can be consumed in the 12th century dining room.

St Andrew's West Hatch:
this little grey Church, with its western tower and pinnacles standing 41 feet high, has a perpendicular chancel and a nave of four bays. It had a north aisle, organ chamber, and south porch. It was rebuilt, along with the tower, in 1861. The north aisle was designed by Mr E Ferry, the County Architect.

There is a small memorial window in the chancel to W.H.P. Gore Langton who died in 1873. The Gore Langtons were leading land owners here. The register dates from 1606.

The church was annexed along with Stoke St Gregory Church to the vicarage at North Curry, under the peculiar jurisdiction of the Dean and Chapter of Wells. It was separated and declared a vicarage on July 10th 1866. In August 1989 a fire swept through the roof of the chancel and the vestry, due, it is thought, to an electrical fault. Local residents formed a human chain to rescue valuables and hymn books and spent the next few days cleaning up the smoke damage. In spite of the fire, services carried on as usual.

There is an interesting board under the tower which explains about the bells, Andrew, Lucy and Mary.

Hatch Beauchamp:
Hatch (Saxon "Hache") means gateway to the forest. When the church was being built the Devil sat on top of Castle Neroche hill and grew angrier and angrier. Eventually he threw a large stone at the church; it fell short and can now be found against the wall of the Hatch Inn. Actually this stone is probably a notch stone. In the days of drove roads and bridle paths which criss-crossed the country, notch stones were put at crossroads so that people could find their way by the number of notches cut in the stone.

A market was once held here, taking place on Thursdays; the licence for it was procured by John de Beauchamp, Lord of the Manor, in 1301. It was discontinued round about the 17th century.

A horse drawn coach called the "Bridport Mail" passed through here, stopping at the Hatch Inn which was a well known coaching inn. The service started from Taunton in the first half of the 19th century. In 1861 an Act of Parliament was passed for the building of a railway line between Taunton and Chard. The Bristol and Exeter Railway Company took up the challenge and so by 1866 this village had its railway station which ran between these two towns. Sadly this also came under the Beeching axe.

The Village had its own Post Office, but the Telegraph Office was at the station.

By 1866 there was a Baptist Chapel, a Wesleyan Chapel and a National School for boys and girls, which also held a Sunday School.

One of the first places that held regular worship by the Baptists was in this village.

By 1906 the village had its own policeman who was called Harry Berry. Two lovely old houses give the village a restaurant known as the Farthings and a home for the elderly known as Hatch Beauchamp Nursing Home.

In recent years there was much concern about the heavy lorries and increased traffic going along the main road which ran through the village, so in the 1980s a new by-pass opened which sent the traffic hurtling away. So Hatch Beauchamp has now become a quiet little backwater.

Hatch Court: after the Norman invasion the Manor of Hatch was given to the Beauchamp family. The line went as follows:

Robert de Beauchamp –	In the reign of Henry II. He paid 17 knights' fees (the extent of an estate which was bound to provide a fully armed knight for the Royal Army, generally was worth about £20 per annum), and he helped to arrange the marriage of Matilda, to Geoffrey of Anjou. He died in 1211.
Robert –	Died age 35 in 1251.
Robert –	Attended the king (Henry III) in his military expedition to France in 1253.
John –	Was appointed by the King (Edward I) to govern the castles of Carmarthen and Cardigan. He died in the twelfth year of the reign.
John –	Knighted with Prince Edward in 1306, before the King's expedition to Scotland. He also obtained a licence for fortifying his Manor House, hereafter called Hatch Castle.
John –	Was one of the Knights who accompanied King

Edward in his wars in France. He was summoned to Parliament from 1336 to 1343, and died that year.

John – Married Alice, daughter of Thomas de Beauchamp, Earl of Warwick (of whose retinue he appeared to be), died without issue in 1361. Left as his co-heirs were Cecilia de Beauchamp, his sister, who was the first wife of Roger Seymour, and John, son of Eleanor Meriet, his other sister. The estate was divided and Cecilia transferred the title of her part of the estate to the Seymours.

The Seymours retained the Manor and, in the reign of Henry VIII, Edward Seymour, Viscount Beauchamp of Hatch, was High Sheriff of Somerset. After his sister Jane had married Henry VIII and then died in childbirth leaving her young son Edward, he became Lord Protector of his nephew on the death of Henry VIII. He was virtually King except in name, and he quarrelled continually with his brother Thomas. Thomas was very kind to the young Princesses, Mary and Elizabeth, Thomas then married Katharine Parr, Henry VIII's last wife, and soon she was pregnant. Edward, still quarrelling with Thomas, accused him of trying to rape the young Princess Elizabeth among other things, and had him executed. Katharine Parr had her baby but died of childbed fever a few weeks later. The Protestant Edward Seymour was executed on Tower Hill on the 22nd January 1552. King Edward died 6th July 1553 aged sixteen, after six years reign. Lady Jane Grey was put on the throne in his place but her reign only lasted nine days, she was then executed. The Catholic Mary then came to the throne.

Hatch Castle fell into disrepair by the year 1633 and in 1676, again by marriage the estate passed to the Bruce family.

In 1755 a fine house was built on the site by Thomas Prowse, architect to John Collins who was then owner of the land. The Collins family were wool merchants and had made their fortune over the past 200 years. John Collins bought extensive land in the area. He went to Oxford and he became High Sheriff of Somerset in 1757.

The new Hatch Court, built in Bath stone, was small but very elegant. It was built in an Italian style and has an arcaded piazza. It is very beautiful. John Collins died in 1792 leaving three sons, who all produced daughters and so the Collins name died out. The House then had many different owners until 1899 when it again fell into disrepair.

It was bought by William Henry Lloyd, a member of the steel and banking family who spent the next twenty years renovating it. He died in 1917. In 1922 Andrew Hamilton Gault married the niece of the widow of

William Lloyd. Hamilton, although born in England, came from a Montreal textile family. His greatest achievement was at the age of 32. He raised and equipped at his own expense a Canadian regiment and brought them to France in 1914. They were the Princess Patricia's Canadian Light Infantry. Hamilton and his wife lived at Hatch Court and in 1931 they bought it. He became M.P. for Taunton in 1924 and held the seat for eleven years until resigning in 1935. He rejoined the Canadian Army as Commandant when World War II started and was appointed Honorary Colonel of the Patricias in 1948 and Colonel of the Regiment in 1956. He died in Montreal in 1958. His name, and information about him, can be found in several places in Taunton, among them the playing fields at Hamilton Road and Galmington Park. Mrs Hamilton Gault lived at Hatch Court until she died in 1972. The house is now owned and occupied by her great-niece and her husband, Dr and Mrs Odgers. They kindly open their lovely house to visitors.

Before leaving Hatch Court, I must mention the grounds, where there is what may well be the smallest deer park in the country. A herd of fallow deer graze in these small grounds and so they are always on view. The day I visited one had just been born and it was the smallest Bambi I have ever seen. A lot of the trees here were sadly lost through Dutch elm disease, but a new replanting programme is under way.

St John the Baptist's Church:

The 40 foot high tower of this church, which stands in the grounds of Hatch Court, is adorned with eight Gothic pinnacles. There are gargoyles (hunky punks) protruding from the tower which are supposed to represent the hunting dogs used in the forest of Neroche. There is an ancient cross in the Church yard.

The painting over the altar is of our Lord being taken down from the cross, with his mother and John the Baptist obviously in the agony of mourning. The picture measuring eight feet by nine and a half feet is in a gilt frame. The register dates from 1760.

The church was restored in 1867. The old organ was removed in 1875 and a superior instrument was purchased by subscription.

John Rose Marriott Chard, hero of Rorke's Drift (1847-1897), won the Victoria Cross for his gallantry when fighting the Zulus. He was a Lieutenant of the Royal Engineers. On 22nd January 1879, 1,000 spear-swinging Zulus had already massacred a whole British battalion at Issandhlwana, when they came upon this small Unit. There were eighty men, thirty five of whom were either wounded or sick, but these gallant men nevertheless resisted the Zulus and eventually the natives withdrew. When Chard came home a banquet was held in his honour and all the silver from the Hatch and North Curry area was used. It was reported as having been a spectacular sight. There is a memorial window to him in this church and he is buried in the churchyard by the south door. He died at only fifty years old. In 1904 a screen of carved oak was placed under the belfry.

Anyone wishing to know more about the de Beauchamps would do well to visit Warwick castle. This branch of the family were the Earls of Warwick. It passed to William de Beauchamp from the Maudit family in 1268. In 1397 Richard II had Thomas de Beauchamp arrested after disagreeing with him over arms. Thomas was thrown into the Tower of London and after that time that particular tower was called the Beauchamp Tower. The origins of Warwick Castle began in Saxon times when Ethelfleda, the daughter of King Alfred the Great, fortified Warwick against the marauding Danes. King Alfred is connected further to this area. One has only to go down the road to Athelney to see King Alfred's monument and in the church at East Lyng one can find out about him burning the cakes and about his famous jewel.

Bickenhall: St Paul's Church, Bickenhall was built in the 15th century.
It was demolished by the Portmans because it was unsafe in 1847. An old Yew Tree and tomb stones mark the spot which is now managed by the Woodland Trust.

A new Bickenhall Church was built in 1849 at the cost of £865. This church is now Neroche Village hall.

Thurlbear: this village is very small but exceptionally pleasant because
of its tall trees. The village school was erected in 1872 for Stoke St Mary and Thurlbear children. The Rev William Lance was the rector here, he was the son of the rector of Buckland St Mary, and he took a large hand in the opening of the school a year later in 1873.

In 1847 one Josiah Daw was sentenced to ten years' transportation as he was found to be one of a group of men who had been stealing sheep and cattle and hiding them in caves on Blagdon Hill.

St Thomas's Church: this ancient Norman style stone structure has
four bells and some rather nice stained glass windows. The register dates from 1700.

The Church is now redundant and is maintained by the Redundant Church Fund. The money for its upkeep is provided by Parliament, the Church and by gifts from the public. Although it is no longer used for regular worship it remains a consecrated building.

The churchyard cross is medieval, no writing can be seen on it, but I noticed that the moulding at the bottom of the shaft is the same design as that of Stoke St Mary's font and doorway, suggesting 15th century. I became very saddened here because in the churchyard near the porch door are the graves of Moses and Mary Chorley and six small gravestones for their children. I tried to imagine the life of Mary Chorley.

Curland: this scattered community has a Methodist Chapel which was built in 1821 by Thomas Murless, owner of the land. It was not registered for marriages until one hundred years later in 1921.

All Saints Church in Curland existed from 900 AD. It was rebuilt as a chapelry for Curry Mallet in the 15th century, hence the name Curry land or Curland. It was rebuilt in 1855 and in 1947 it was taken over by Staple Fitzpaine. The last service was held here in 1970 and by 1989 it was sadly up for sale as a private residence. After it closed as a church it was used by the County Museum as a store. The altar table has gone to Staple Fitzpaine.

It was near here, at a farm called Dead Man's Post, that a father murdered his son. The man was always so cruel to the boy and one day when the twelve-year-old was kneeling in the earth doing some work, his father hit him so hard that he rolled over into the ditch, never to rise again. Neighbours working with him witnessed this, and saw the father pick the child up like a dog and carry him home. There he put him to bed with three other children, but in the morning the boy was dead. The father was convicted of murder.

Whitestaunton: within the grounds of the Manor House is an old Roman villa, which was discovered in 1882 by the owner, and St. Agnes's well. This spring reputedly has medicinal properties.

Nearby is Horse Pool Copse, where there is a prehistoric earthwork, known as Whitestaunton Camp.

St. Andrew's Church: the Norman font is the only relic that would suggest a church was on this site in those days. This church was built in 1483 and finished in 1492. The De Stauntons were given this heritage but it passed to the Bretts and the Hugyns, probably through marriage; they were the families who built the church.

Simon Brett in his will dated 1530 asked to be buried at the foot of the high altar.

There are memorials to the Brett family in the north chapel; in the south chapel are memorials to the Elton family of the Manor from 1768 onwards. Lt. Col Fred. C. Elton, who won a Victoria Cross in the Crimean War, is also buried in this Church.

There are six funeral hatchments hanging in the chancel and south chapel, one belonging to a member of the Brett family, undated, and five more to members of the Elton family.

The fine rood screen is of the perpendicular period and remains of the rood stair in the north side of the nave can still be seen.

There are five bells in the tower, two of which are pre-Reformation. The pews have nicely carved bench ends.

The 1930 organ was installed by Colonel and Mrs Mitchell of the Manor, It was blown by hand until 1956, when their children gave a new electric blower as a memorial to their parents.

Chard: the Romans built a road through here and there was a Saxon settlement, but the town was founded in 1234 by Bishop Jocelyn of Wells. On each side of its main street there is a running stream, which is unusual in that the one on the north side runs into the Bristol Channel and that on the south side runs into the English Channel.

There was a great fire of Chard in 1577. Most of the houses would have been built mainly of wood at this time. That is probably why the oldest building is the old Grammar School dated 1583. In the Civil War of 1644-45, Blake tried to hold Taunton for the Parliamentarians and King Charles held a Council at Chard to discuss ways in which Taunton could be taken.

The Museum is a 17th century house. There is a section here devoted to the work of John Gillingham who, in the 19th century, was the first man ever to make artificial limbs.

John Stringfellow was another Chard character. He was the first man to fly a power driven aeroplane in 1847, and his model can still be seen in London's Science Museum.

Choughs Hotel (named after the bird) is reputed to be haunted. There are at least three different ghost stories here, two of them being voices in the passage, and of the old man sitting in the chair by the fire being Judge Jeffreys, first Baron of Wem. Readers would do well to call here and hear the stories for themselves.

The Baptist Chapel was erected in 1842. The Chard Canal Company was founded in 1834. It built a canal to Creech St Michael, where it joined the Bridgwater Canal. It was bought out in 1866 by the Bristol and Exeter Railway Company.

The Railway came to Chard when Chard Road Station was opened by the London and South Western Railway on 19th July 1860 on the Exeter to Yeovil line. In 1863 a short line was opened from here to Chard Basin about three miles away, this was the point where the canal reached the town. These lines were all of standard gauge. Chard Road was later renamed Chard Junction and Chard Basin renamed Chard Town.

On September 11th 1866 another line was opened from Taunton to Chard which went into a new station called Chard Joint. This was run by the B. & E.R. and was a broad gauge line. The L.S.W.R. joined up Chard Town with Chard Joint (which were about half a mile apart) by building sidings and loops of both gauges. This meant that the L.S.W.R. could run

97

services to all three stations. The line to Taunton was changed to standard gauge in 1891. From December 30th 1916 the G.W.R. took over the line through to Chard Junction and Chard Town was closed.

All these trains would of course have been pulled by steam engines and the Railway Companies received numerous claims from people who lived adjacent to the line and had their washing burnt by sparks flying from the engines.

With Nationalisation and the establishment of British Rail in 1947, Chard Joint station was renamed Chard Central. The last line was closed on September 10th 1962, with the Beeching axe.

Toll roads once covered the main roads of the county and the coming of the canals saw the end for many of these, likewise the railways gave the canals a short-lived life. Now canals are coming back into their own as tourist attractions.

Another of Chard's main industries was glove making. The Georgian Guildhall in the centre of the town with its lovely columns displays inside some lovely paintings done by the pupils of Holyrood School. They depict various aspects of Chard's history from the Great Fire to the recent twinning with a town in France.

There is a golf course on Windwhistle Hill and also the large park of Cricket St Thomas three miles to the east.

St Mary the Virgin: this was a Norman church but the only remaining effect now is a Norman arch in the chancel wall. It is in perpendicular style with a wagon roof.

John Stringfellow is buried in the Churchyard. There is an interesting memorial to William Brewer, Surgeon, dated 1614, and his wife and eleven children.

In 1986 some concern was expressed by mourners returning to inspect flowers after the funerals and finding galvanised iron placed across the graves, with the flowers on top. There appeared to be a shortage of grave diggers to fill in these new graves.

Hornsbury Mill: the mill was built in 1830 and was still in full production in 1942. The miller's lavatory is worth a look; it is an overshot (the water comes over the top) mill wheel. The mill is now a restaurant and a museum.

Forde Abbey: Founded in 1138 and nearing completion by 1142, it housed twelve Cistercian Monks. The building is preserved as one of the most perfect Cistercian Houses left.

The last abbot was Thomas Chard, who himself built and maintained the Great Hall. After the Dissolution it was turned into a private residence and Sir Edmund Prideaux carried out a few alterations. Mainly what can be seen however is much as it was in those early days.

The Abbey is set in thirty acres of grounds on the south side of the river Axe. One can walk around the lakes and gardens. There are picnic areas laid out with tables. There is also an Abbey shop.

Here there are seventy acres of extra ground where people can pick their own fruit.

In the house can be seen the famous Mortlake Tapestries, which were made by Flemish workers in a factory founded by King Charles I.

Combe St Nicholas: An old lamp post and a tree stand on the Village green as a memorial to 60 years of Queen Victoria's reign.

The Manor of Combe St Nicholas was given to Giso, Bishop of Wells, in 1070.

Another Bronze Age barrow is nearby at Combe Beacon.

In the 19th century Betty Trump, a young girl of 14, was murdered between here and Buckland St Mary where she was visiting her grandma. She had her windpipe severed. The body was found several days later in a wood.

The public house is the Green Dragon.

St Nicholas's Church: the Church was built in 1237 on the site of a previous place of worship. It was restored in the 15th century in the perpendicular style, but Norman work can still be seen in the north doorway. The rood screen was carved in 1480 and was restored in 1921. It was put together by village carpenters from the remains of the old one. One of the bells is 400 years old.

The main family name here is Bonners. There are two fonts, one 15th century and the other 900 years old.

There is a small museum in the corner.

Castle Neroche: this prehistoric hill fort was given to Count Robert of Mortain by his half brother, William the Conqueror. He made the old earth work site into a Norman stronghold with deep ditches.

Here was once a Royal Forest. In the days of hunting laws, the hare was protected. Fallow deer were introduced into Neroche. In the 1620s Charles I needed to raise money for the Navy, so he set about deforestation. Neroche came under that axe and at the time it was under the care of the Poulettes. The land was divided up, one third for the Lord of the Manor, one third common rights and one third for the King. Poulett stirred up the local people against this and was rebuked by the King. In 1634 King Charles sold off his third of land which was bought mainly by the Portmans. Commoners were given the poor land in their third share and so

99

got the worst of the deal. Just along the road from here was the Castle Inn, Buckland St Mary. It is no longer an inn but a private dwelling. It was at this inn in the 19th century that the trial took place of the Curland farmer who murdered his son. They lived at Dead Man's Post.

The viewpoint on Castle Neroche is 870 feet above sea level and from here on a clear day you can see Sedgemoor where the vicious and bloody battle took place.

There are some oak trees in this forest which were saplings six hundred years ago. It is the sheer undeveloped characteristics of these hills which give them their beauty.

So my walk is complete. It now feels rather flat, very much like when the children left home. I hope the facts are all accurate, I have tried to check everything two or three times. I have met many lovely people during the past two years on the hills, I just wish I could name them all and thank them.

Acknowledgements

My thanks and acknowledgements go to the following:
Kelly's *Directory of Somerset*.
John Collinson (1791).
A Book of Taunton by Robin Bush.
The Devon and Somerset Blackdowns by Ronald Webber.
David Bromwich and Taunton Records Office; Taunton Museum.
The Church and House Guides.
The many parishioners who have given their time to tell me unusual stories about their villages.
A Dictionary of British Social History by L.W. Cowie.
My husband for walking and helping.
Stan Gwyther for reading this book upon completion.